The
BACHELORETTE
PARTY DANCER

Keep Hope Alive... Don't Give up

A story for young people to learn about the challenges of
life in the Big City

Jason Cool

Foreword

We all face challenges growing up. However, learning from our mistakes and passing the honest truth on will prevent others from making the same mistakes; that is the purpose of this book. This is a lifelong goal of mine: to pass on the knowledge I have learned. As I was growing up, I always felt that this would be my purpose, and I asked for a safe passage through the dark side of life to be able to tell you first-hand why it does or does not work. I do prefer to walk in the light and have my intentions on display for everyone to know right off the bat. I hope this method of writing will be easy for you to understand and follow. If you are young or old, I hope to keep your attention, because I know that my attention was directed to pleasure and fun for most of my life.

I am 35 years old now and still feel like I am 25 years old. I lived most of my life doing exactly what I wanted because I did not realize that what I wanted at the time was not the best thing for my life. All I knew was I had a talent, and I wanted to explore the potential of my abilities even if it was a risk to my health or future. I had a feeling that I would share what I learned with the world, and I hoped the world would take the time to understand my creative and slightly original life story.

I ask you, do you know what you want to do for the next 20 years of your life? Do you have any experience in that field right now? Most of us have an idea of what we want to become if we are lucky. Others may only know that they want a college education, so that way they can choose later what they want to become. I wanted to be a light in a dark place. I wanted to be able to tell people, why, from first-hand experience, from true stories that happened in today's world, so that they could understand in clear reason to do or not do a particular activity. I was raised in a religious home, so most of the advice I received came in very strict terms. My father would say, "It's a sin, God doesn't want you to have sex before marriage, you will go to hell." These were some of the answers I received that I did not comprehend. This left me in a very dimly lit room of answers and did not satisfy my curiosity.

I needed real examples. This book is based on a true story; however, for storytelling purposes, names have been changed and will remain fictional. Working as a hair stylist, I have learned that my personal stories shared while working have created the biggest bonds with my friends and clients. Being able to share the truth has created trust and value and has given me the purpose for my life. I love to give, and giving my story will help people. When I have more to give to the world, I will be ready and willing to share as much as I can with as many as I can. Please read this book any way you like. I created chapters that you can read out of sequence and still learn. It is difficult for me to sit down and read a book that does not keep my attention. As I got older, documentaries became my favorite form of education. I do hope to turn this book into a film.

Reading these stories, you will have answers to questions you may not know you have. You will gain a perspective of how this young man's world works. My goal is for you not to make the same mistakes I have. Keep your hope alive, and do not give up on yourself. Too many times, I lost hope and felt worthless, and not until I realized that I had created a good life for myself and lived and learned. I stayed strong.

I do have the potential to build my life the way I always dreamt it to be. I simply had to share my life with you.

Acknowledgements

With deepest gratitude, I wish to thank:

My father, for teaching me by example the discipline I learned as a child, that stayed with me my whole life. Without his example, I could not have made it. Thank you for believing in me.

My mother, the only woman who truly loves me in weakness and in strength, who always believed in me and, by pure love, picked me up off the ground to live when I felt hopeless.

Drewski, my brother from another mother, I would not have survived LA without you, bro.

Amber, the girl I loved so much for so long, who grew up with me and showed me true love and gave me a fantasy that is my reality. My competition, an inspiration, someone I wish the best. Old flames are remembered dearly.

Mr Big, who gave me hope and allowed me to feel valuable when I was at my lowest point in life. Safely getting me through the roughest part of my life.

Mrs. Big, for her love and support, whose wisdom and knowledge let me into Beverly Hills and gave me a reason to stand on my own two feet again. I will get back to the plush life in LA. The bad girls for being bad and being really good at it. The memories are more priceless than gold. Living my fantasy and making it my reality.

To my Guardian Angels that came into my life when I needed you, you saved me from the feelings that led to actions that would not be the real me. Life is a balance. I hope I found it.

Table of Contents

Introduction

The Bachelorette Dancer - *Keep Hope Alive... Don't Give Up* is here to save my life and your life. Its purpose is to help you and me realize that we are all connected. My experience can benefit your life experiences, so you will not feel the pain and suffering that I have. Also, it's a guide to help you feel the pleasures of life that we are supposed to be able to feel. My biggest concern growing up as a kid was that everyone knows we are young, and we are going to be tempted to do the things we are told we shouldn't. Why is there not a guide to tell us if you plan to break the rules? Here is how you should do it. Since I know you and I are going to do what we want to do, there should be some kind of open-source knowledge that will guide you from really destroying your opportunities, and by being open and honest with you, you may be able to resist the temptations. This is just my story with things changed to make it fictional.

I was born in a world right before the technology boom. I was alive when the world did not have pagers, cell phones, or the internet. It is incredible to me the changes I have seen the world go through already. I would like to reach people who are just starting to become adults, young people who are just now realizing that they have the power to create their world by the choices they decide to make. I really started to feel like an adult in sixth grade. I feel like this book should be read by anyone who wants to know what it's like to live a wild life. *Keeping Hope Alive* is here for anyone who has taken a risk in life that left them vulnerable and emotionally weak. Maybe it was your parents who took that risk, and you are feeling the repercussions.

I will take you through my world of being a model, going to auditions for TV commercials, living in the big city, breaking your mother's and father's hearts, healing from the mistakes you have made, healing from being hungover from drinking too much, religion, the purpose for your life, and how to be a bad and good lover. These are just a few topics that will be covered.

Childhood Expectations

The first chapter is about the world I grew up in, how my parents shaped my expectations out of daily life, and how I started to realize that I was the only one who had control of creating the world I wanted, desired, and deserved. We are the sum of all our actions, choices, and the days we have lived. Every time we cry, every bite of cake we eat, every time we succeed, all of these add up to become our own feelings about ourselves. This is the most important realization of ourselves because these are the reasons we are who we are and feel the way we do.

Each chapter will take you closer and closer to how I became an adult, which I did not want to become. Although living on my own and paying my own bills doesn't make me an adult. Well, it does, but I still see myself as a young man who loves to live life without a job. I want to be a kid forever. Although I have learned there is a time and place for work, I have to give back to the world; my time has come, and I am ready. My goal is to make sure you are ready as well when your time comes to wake up and go create something beautiful you are proud of.

We have many choices to decide, what to post and what not to post on Instagram, what parties to go to, and who to dance with. All of these choices will have an impact on your life. I had made some poor choices in my life that left me hopeless, and I gave up on myself, too many times, feeling worthless and unlovable. I like to think of myself now as living in the middle. I wasn't living in poverty, and I wasn't living like a billionaire. Technically, it's not the top or the bottom but somewhere in between.

Chasing fun was the majority of my youth, not the best decision; I wish I had had the power to stay home and work, go to night school, study study study. This is the advice I would give my little sister, who is a freshman in high school right now. I tell her life doesn't really start till you get to college. College is where you live outside of your parents' realm. After you have graduated from high school, you are legal and able to make your own decisions as an 18-year-old. This is the beginning of you on your own terms if you choose.

This is the Danger Zone, and this is where *Keep Hope Alive* will help you make the decisions that you feel are right for you. Allowing you to have some glimpse into my life, I hope you will see that I have tried everything I could think of to become a successful creative millionaire. I was a wild child who had no plan for the future because of my family dysfunction. I wanted to live for today, because that is all I could see at the time. I wanted to have the coolest life, and I had no idea what kind of ride I was going to be in for, SMH. That is not how I started out. I fell into this path because I lost hope in my family, and I gave up on believing in their advice. I had myself, and this was a lonely environment. I told myself that as long as I am happy, that is all that matters. At the time, it was better than dealing with all the fighting my family was doing, not being able to agree on anything. You will see that no matter how many times I gave up, I always came back to believing in myself. Hope could come back to me and shed light on my life.

I always chose to listen to hope and cultivate it and keep it alive until I found the secret to my success.

What I love is the purpose of my life. I know what I love because when I feel love, I feel happy and complete. I feel that there is no other place in the universe that I should be than right here doing what I love. Sometimes what we love will change, and we have to allow that to happen. Typically, it changes on its own, and we have to accept it because we cannot change it. Not saying it can't come back either. Okay, let's get started. I hope I have your attention, and you can follow my reading. This will take you through so many wild stories that I am not sure how I survived.

My life's goal now is to find my true self without the restriction of money. I want to travel the world and create documentaries that change the way Americans vote. I want to fall in love and have that bloom into many wonderful years together. I want to start a few companies that allow people to discover/live their dreams to their fullest potential here on Earth. I would love to free my fellow friends from the boxes they live in. If you are unhappy with your life, I want to help show you the way to happiness. I want to create a sober place where creative people can meet and openly express themselves on multiple levels. One day, I will buy a house and have a family, and that is my goal.

Childhood Expectations

As human beings, we are incredibly complex with an endless stream of physical, emotional, mental, and spiritual needs that must be satisfied. I remember this specific story that my mother had told me about myself as a child. My character as a young person has pretty much stayed with me my whole life. When I was a few months old, I was placed in my crib, a place to keep me safe. In my crib, I would see my mother pass by, and I would put my arms out reaching for her attention, reaching for success, reaching for the person who loved me most in life. Many times, my mother would come to me and take care of me; that was all I needed, like most of us. As I got older, she knew I could go longer periods of time without her constant attention. Without my consent, my mother would walk past me, and sometimes she would not have time to pay attention to me. This is where I would toss myself back in disbelief, falling to the safety of my cushioned crib, crying and feeling pain. It was like the world was over, just because I couldn't get her attention. She was my world at that time.

This same type of emotional behavior would become more complex as life went on. I believe we draw our conclusions about life from our experiences. We may feel like we know what our purpose in life is; if you do, that is incredible. You should pursue that dream till you attain your life's goal. I would venture to say that most people do not have a specific idea of what our purpose is. We do a wide variety of experimenting to discover ourselves. This is such an important part of our development.

As a child, my expectations were quite simple, I suppose. I had two older brothers, who took care of me; they were my guardian angels. My mother and father provided most of my needs. We had a normal upbringing for the most part. From birth till about six years old, I don't have too many memories that I can recall. Although looking back, I can say that I did not know that, subconsciously, what I expected from my family, I did receive.

I expected that my family would have a house, with rent or mortgage paid by my parents, every month, and food would be prepared for me every day, 3 times a day. My parents would go to work five days a week, and as children, all these things happened. I was lucky my dad was responsible. I have always had that opinion of my father because he has always had strict discipline for himself and all that he does. He did his best to pass that quality on to us as children. We had no clue how challenging it is to be successful adults and what our parents had to go through to get to where they are. We just wanted to be taken care of and allowed to explore the world at our leisure, as most kids do.

I have this very clear memory of being a baby, still in my diaper, just barely learned how to walk on my own two feet. It was a sunny day in California. I was with my mother outside in the sunshine playing in the water from the sprinkler, having the time of my life, so happy, not a care in the world. That was the day I met my first honey bee. Little did I know of this honey bee's power and self-protection. I made the mistake of thinking that I was bigger than the bee and I could step on it with no problems. That was when I felt the pain of a stinger on my baby foot. That memory has stayed with me my whole life. I repeated that mistake in many ways in my adult life. I had to learn to respect the bee, for the bee is an important part of the cycle of life on Earth as we know it. I was not expecting that bee; I had no idea it even existed. Obviously, pain is one of the greatest lessons we will learn; if it causes us pain, we will want to stay away from this thing that causes us pain.

All in all, that is the purpose of finishing this book: I would love to allow you to avoid the pain that I experienced. Secondly, this book will cover the details of situations we may find ourselves in today's world. I call it "hot girl problems" or "toxic male behavior." The book my parents gave me was the Bible to learn from. Needless to say, I barely read it or parts of it because I had to, not because I wanted to or understood the basic principles, or could adapt it to today's world. Maybe I should have paid more attention to the Bible, and my life wouldn't have had so many twists and turns. As a child, I felt like I had all my needs met. Once my parents divorced, everything went downhill fast. At least, looking back on it today, I feel like I did have good times with my needs met. I strongly urge you to let go of the past, heal from it, and move to the future where we are today. Only what you do today will set you up for tomorrow. We build brick by brick the house we live in, just as this book is being written page by page, word by word, letter by letter.

I was enrolled in a private school, starting out in preschool. Both my parents worked, so we had early morning daycare and preschool, then after-school daycare. My parents did not become rich or wealthy. They did not break free from the norms of society. My father did not take risks. He was from a small town in Pennsylvania and, due to his Christian beliefs, did not want to become wealthy. I remember the days before preschool. My mother would take me around with her throughout the day. Back then, she designed flower arrangements for weddings. We would go downtown to the flower mart and choose flowers. She would ask me what I thought, and just laugh and say that I was cute. I do remember my mother occasionally having a bit of road rage. She would fight back, and this became part of me as well. To satisfy your curiosity, my mother would cuss and flick off people who were jerk drivers. Little me did not understand that it was not okay for her to do this. She did not want me to copy her road rage energy, and when I did, I would get in trouble. Honestly, this created lots of confusion in me because this contradictory behavior didn't make sense to me. I saw my mother getting angry at a driver, and I wanted to defend my mother. It was a natural instinct for me.

I choose to live my life in the natural instinct world. I want to follow my heart, my body, and my mind. I don't want to read books that tell me what to do. I want to read books that tell me how it is. That's why I love documentaries, and that's why I film as much of my life as I can today. The endless search for truth and wisdom with a scientific explanation of how and why the world is the way it is will satisfy my mind. That is why I HAD to take these risks. I took risks to get a first-hand explanation and a first-hand experience for myself. I feel like I can safely say I took more risks than most people I have ever met. I did not think I would live past 30 years old. Maybe I just never imagined being that old. Writing this book is a risk. It may not sell (I feel it will do good). I will have expressed the life experiences I went through. I will have to relive all these experiences in my head as I write and edit. What do I have to lose? Nothing. That is why I took all these chances in the first place. I felt like I had nothing to lose because I did not see the value in the advice my parents gave me after they had failed me by getting a divorce when I was only 6 years old. This broke me in half. I stopped believing in a God named Jesus. I prayed and prayed for them to get back together. So, I also lost value in myself, which led to many more heartbreaks, due to my own instability and lack of belief or rules.

So, for the most part, preschool had prepared me for regular school, K-6. Looking back on those days, I realized I had a bit of dyslexia. I didn't even really understand what that was back then. My nines became sixes. My B's became D's. I soon realized that math and science, and physical education were my strongholds. I was at the top of my class in being brave. I was a leader, and I always wanted to be first, either because I am an Aries or because I have to show off, I don't know exactly. My brothers used to joke about being a martyr. That is what I am, and they were so correct about me. Because we were in a private school, we had a stricter education. My brothers would teach me anything I did not know. I had the greatest time in the world pretending; with them getting laughs, it was heaven having them. However, we would get in trouble for having too much fun sometimes. Have you ever been sitting at the dinner table, and anytime you looked into your siblings' eyes, laughter would just keep pouring out for some inside joke? That was one of my favorite memories. My parents said to stop laughing and eat our dinner. I would look down and try to pull myself together. As soon as I looked up again, I would burst out in laughter, and we got in trouble that night. I guess we just needed to calm down at the dinner table. Aw, good times.

Second Grade & Third Grade

I vividly remember my sex drive waking up and becoming a reality. This girl named Allison was in my class, and I was so in love with her that she definitely got two Valentine's Day cards with candy from me, accidentally on purpose. Fast-forwarding briefly 20-plus years to the future, I was in Walnut Creek, California, at this club, and I ran into the same Allison. I was like, 'Omg! Allison, it's me,' and she remembered me, of course.

It was her Bachelorette party, and she was getting married soon. Luckily, I was obviously over her by then lol. I felt so lucky to see her before she got married. I had so much more life to live before I got married. Will I ever get married? I don't know. I had plans to leave Earth and float in outer space before I settled down. I am a wild soul, I am a rule breaker, I am a risk taker, and a dreamer. The point was that my childhood expectations changed. I thought as a kid that I needed her approval. I needed her to love me, and when the day came that it was her last night of being single, I had zero attraction to her. This means something to me: my innocence as a child had no connection to the future I was bound to experience. What I thought I wanted and what the world told me I needed was far from what my heart, mind, body, and soul would lead me to.

My third-grade teacher was so hot. She always wore amazing clothes. Her makeup was pretty flawless, and she was so classy. We had one teacher for all the subjects we studied at the private Christian school I went to. It's just amazing to me that we, as conscious beings, have feelings at such a young age. We are shaped by our experiences. We get jaded by pain, and we become numb to feelings. We become callous to pain. Needless to say, third grade passed by very quickly, and I was on to fourth grade. I partially remember my fourth-grade teacher being a balding male who wasn't quite as interesting to listen to or watch. That's all I remember as of now. Oh yeah, around then, I was letting my hair grow in what was cool back then. I had a tail, as they called it. Being in a private school, they made me cut it off. I was too cool for school and would express my individuality. Around this time, my school thought we were old enough for the D.A.R.E. program. I do remember enjoying the time of learning the regular class schedule.

Drugs were explained to us, although they didn't really explain them to us. I had a general understanding, but seriously, I had no clue. I just had a vague idea that they were dangerous. A lot of people would become addicted and possibly ruin their lives permanently. They did instill a fear of crack, cocaine, heroin, and PCP. Aids was still a new disease that put a lot of fear into me. We were just young kids, and they used pain/fear to steer us away from these chemically addictive substances. I am grateful and thankful because I didn't dedicate my life to any of these substances. This fear would guide me during my teenage years and my adult life.

Fifth Grade

We are old kids, almost young adults. Nothing about 5th grade, do I really remember? Just this was the year that I would end private school and be let go into public school with all the kids of the city. I was ready to start the 6th grade in middle school. I should bring up the fact that my private school had an annual fundraiser. We would sell chocolate bars to raise money. This was one of my favorite times of the year. We had contests to see who would sell the most, and it was so much fun eating the chocolate.

I loved collecting money. I felt so powerful and so adult-like. I was a young businessman. I could sell a chocolate bar for $2, and that would allow me to eat one myself. Plus, we, as young kids, could walk outside on our own from door to door, exploring our world and city. I was very good at starting conversations. I had no fear. I do remember walking through the hallways of my new public school each year, passing by the pretty girls whom I was so attracted to. I had to learn to overcome my fear of talking to girls, and it was like stage fright. This was a lifelong goal of mine as a kid. I had tried over and over again to speak, and no words would come out. I would walk near the girls and be taken over by fear or embarrassment for no logical reason. One summer, I came back to school with a vengeance, something like the Revenant that should win me an Oscar for my performance.

I vaguely remember my first run. I was talking to one of the older girls, and she was perfect to me. I had to do it. I had to use what I learned from selling chocolates door to door: just keep talking, say what you need to say, and wait.

That magical day came to me at a young age. They accepted me. I felt loved and respected, and I was let into a world where the girls, who would become my favorite energy in the whole world, I was granted a golden ticket. I was in eternal bliss. That drug was released in my brain, and I would never get enough. The pain of not doing it and the fear of rejection became so secondary that the risk was worth it to me.

This lesson would last me a lifetime. This lesson would be the basis of life for me. I made a small fortune off this lesson. Selling chocolate at a profit to me personally and talking to pretty girls were the major lessons I took with me from this school. I would look back on the nice guy that going to a private school taught me to be, and being the nice guy unless you are talking to a nice girl means nothing. I live in LA; we have a strong urge to succeed, and by all means, the man and woman who take care receive care. Demand your life, get in touch with yourself, and make your dreams a reality. You need to realize that your childhood expectations can be completely false and mean nothing to you today. What you thought you wanted as a kid doesn't have to hold you back from what you want today. Just because you loved it when you were young doesn't mean that it will make you happy today. One of the most important parts of my life included breaking my mother's heart and telling my father that I do not want to be like you; I will not follow your beliefs. I take the best of both my parents and allow those qualities to live inside me. I do love my parents. I admire both of them greatly in the long run. I became similar to both of my parents. Very strict like my father, and very wild like my mother. I am two-sided like a coin, although one side does take persistence.

Public School Teenager

Welcome to sixth grade. I was no longer in private school, and my parents were divorced. I was so fresh on the scene, it was ridiculous. Coming from my old school, I had no enemies. I wasn't ready. I did not realize people would be against me, even though I hadn't done anything to them. Suddenly, I was in a whole new competition.

Over that 5th-grade summer, I was introduced to Pot Drinking. I was really good at shoulder-tapping for beers. People always liked me for the most part, and I could always be polite and naturally charming.

I had met this one guy when I was shoulder-tapping beers for my brothers. He asked me if I needed anything else, like pot, etc. I took his number and kept it. As the school year continued, I realized that my education level was above everyone else's. My private school had taught us quicker, and I let that get to me. One day, it caught up with me.

I had my older brother with me at my middle school. My oldest brother was in the 9th grade, and he hated the change from private school to public. He decided to take his G.E.D. and graduate early, 6 months into ninth grade. I wish I was that intelligent. Instead, my way of finding success was having money to buy myself candy in the morning before having to get on the school bus. See, the local store had candy that the cafeteria did not have. During class, people would see me eating these candies, and I became the candy man. I would buy candy for 5 cents and sell it for 25 cents—Lemonheads, Warheads, and Airheads.

The sexiest girl in my class came up to me and asked me to be her boyfriend. I was a Christian boy who did not know what had just happened. It was a surprise, but nevertheless, it felt great. I loved it. I didn't know who she was, and I had never even really seen her before. The shocker was when she came up to me, and I was totally unprepared.

I said yes to her because she was everything I was attracted to. We were popular, and I had no idea what I was supposed to do with this girl. Looking back, she must have been really experienced. Additionally, she also had a fully developed Latin girl's pretty face. She made an impact on my mind; granted, I still remember her today. A few things happened here. After maybe 2 weeks of dating her, she asked me to kiss her. I was such a kid, so I kissed her on the cheek.

She, looking back, wanted an ass grab and full French kiss, which I wanted to do, but just didn't have the balls to do it yet. Now, this kid, who I considered a close friend at the time, who could look like my younger brother, asked me why I was dating her. I told him that I didn't know. She had asked me out, and that was it. She was pretty, so that was an added bonus.

I remember him saying, "Yeah, she's a loser and a slut. You should break up with her, so I did."

Two days later, he was dating her, LMFAO. This was the 1st lesson in public school, B.S.

What a trip down memory lane.

People will stab you in the back in your youth and ignorance. It's kind of incredible how fast we switched from being good old Christian boys to the real world. My middle brother and I decided it would be a good idea to be part of the cool kids. We were a force to be reckoned with, and we had the hottest girls after us. We were tall, confident, good at sports, and had a better education than the other kids.

So, the local kids had a gang that we decided we wanted to be part of. The only way in was to get jumped in. We had to fight all the kids at the same time by ourselves. This was to prove to ourselves that we had the balls to fight and stand up to anyone.

I remember seeing them go after my brother. He was doing well at first, fighting 5 or 6 kids at the same time. He was pushed up against the fence, crouched down, and was getting beaten. As far as my memory goes, I ran over and pushed them all away. I blindsided them, then they stopped, and it was my turn to fight. I can't say I remember any of it, but we survived. Now, we had this shared traumatic experience with those kids, and that created a bond that made us feel closer. I vaguely remember going with them all to buy 40s (Beer) after the fight. We were all like brothers now. It was kind of scary to me at the time.

I certainly did not trust these kids, and I always felt like they were jealous of me and my brother. It was a cutthroat competition for king of the hill, and the kid who stole my girl was in the gang, too. I didn't know what I had lost, nor did I know what to do about it. My training was in a Christian School. I was taught to be kind to my neighbor, to turn the other cheek when I was wronged, and to forgive and forget to be the bigger person. So much of that advice would screw me over as a kid. My forced Christian education would give me the nature to be kind and timid, and see how things panned out. I was always nice at first. However, this doesn't always equate to success in the real world.

After we got the beers, it was all fun and games. That same day, I still had my heavy backpack on. I didn't want to carry it anymore. On the way to the Ice Creamery, where we played video games, I left my bag with a complete stranger at the bus stop. I had no reason to leave my most valuable belongings with a complete stranger, other than that I was drunk and not thinking clearly. The next day, I woke up and didn't have any of my school supplies. I was pretty much screwed. What a horrible day. All of that went to waste. Just a perfectly good student making bad decisions. Luckily, the lady I left my backpack with turned it in at the local store across the street, which was a stationery supply store. The store contacted my school, which then called me into the office.

This was the beginning of my young adult life, the adrenaline rush of being aggressive and drinking. I felt like a boss. I felt like I was above the other normal kids; I was part of an elite team that ran the school. As I naturally should be, back in Christian school, I was the leader of my class.

I was always challenged by authority and wanted to be the leader of anything I was part of. I quickly discovered the feeling of being at the top of the social class in my small world in 6th grade. As most kids do, we all hung out after school, drinking at a girl's party and a pot. We all loved it. This was 1992-1993. Dr. Dre, the original Chronic, was playing, Eazy-E was still alive, and Ice Cube was on the radio singing. Today was a good day. I still had the phone number to the guy who had asked me if I needed anything else besides beer.

For my 13th birthday, I decided it would be a good Idea to buy a gram of cocaine. Before then, I was getting 1/8's of weed, a half oz. My candy-selling days became drugs. Our clothes had changed from preppy pretty boys to Ben Davis and Dickies. I was the first in my family to have a pager and a cell phone. I was living with my mother, and we had free rein to be whoever we wanted to be. She was now married to an alcoholic, whom I will call Mr. C, and the fighting was endless a futile. Because I was living with my mother, and my 13th birthday came around, it was time to see my dad - the one I had left when I moved out of his house.

I undermined all of his teachings to me and turned my back on him as much as I could; his teachings made me a wimp, a loser. I wanted to fight for my manhood. I wanted to beat the system. I would have done anything to have my family back together, and this was the only other substitute. My dad came and picked me up and asked where I wanted to go for my birthday. I said, "Pizza," and off we went. I thought I was so cool for having cocaine on me and being high, and my father didn't even know. What a bad idea. Lost in the world.

Later that night, I went to hang out with my gang of friends.

I was set up when I arrived at the school playground of a local elementary school, where we would drink and smoke. A guy who wanted my position was jealous of me and wanted to prove his superiority. He claimed he had good reason to fight me. I was nervous and on edge, since the cocaine and adrenaline were intense. I still remember the feeling. They were giving us knives to fight with, but I kept on denying the fight and saying we had no reason to fight. Soon, I would realize that there was no other option but to fight. With my heart pounding, feeling the intimidation of being confronted, knowing I had to prove myself, my brother was not with me, the elder gang members wanted us to fight, and I had no way out. I chose to win. With my first punch, I threw a right hook, and it landed. He was bleeding and didn't really fight back. I was vindicated. I was celebrated. My brothers threw their arms around me and gave me their drinks, offered me a cigarette to smoke, and passed the weed to me.

This feeling came up in my life so many other times, as you will see, not feeling like I had any other chance but to fight, to give my last ounce of hope, and put everything on the line. I either win or lose. Here it is. The world is watching.

I created my first hater. I hated him, and I'm sure he hated me. He never caused me any other problems, that I know of, although protecting myself and the paranoia would affect me. I wanted to feel safe, so I bought a double-bladed knife, which I took with me everywhere. One day, we all drove out to San Francisco to go to the strip club. On the way home, my friend was driving, and she was a little drunk. The cops came and pulled us over. I knew that this knife was illegal to have, and I freaked out.

I stashed it in the car, then I put it back in my bag. As the officer was checking the car, he asked to check my bag. That was the first time I went to jail. It was either the driver or me, and I didn't want her to pay for my mistake. Although looking back, I should have let her take the fall; the police wouldn't even look in between the seats where I was planning to stash it. I got my first taste of harsh reality. I had the fear of jail now in my mind. Lucky I did because I couldn't stand being locked up. I will never do anything that could land me in that situation. I just can't take it. I can't be around men locked up. There are very few males that I will ever allow myself to trust.

Especially being locked up with criminals. No offense to anyone reading this—it's just that I'd rather be in my clean house, with my clean girlfriend, able to eat whatever I want, sleep when I want, drink when I feel like it, watch what I want, and hit the beach whenever I please.

I barely graduated from 9th grade. I was caught with a Marijuana pipe on me at school. Lucky I had sold all that skunk weed right before I was busted. I was sent to a continuation school. I was knee deep in being the cool kids now. I came up with the slogan, "You have the sniffles," which meant you have been doing nose candy. I had what you needed or wanted. I was among the damaged now. I was known. No guessing, I was a bad kid now. We used to smoke weed in class and blow it out the door when the teacher had her back to us. Everyone in continuation school had parents who could no longer control their kids. We were taking acid, and losing our minds, taking speed. We lived in San Leandro, which is right next to Oakland. House music and raves were just coming to life now. My oldest brother forced us to listen to the new style of music we didn't want to. Now we love it. Speed Racer was one of the songs I really remember listening to. We also had watched behind the mind's eye and tripped out. It was quite an interesting time to be on the scene.

We had drifted so far from our natural paths, from being in private schools to public schools. Our futures were dramatically altered for all three of us brothers. Over the summer, my middle brother moved in with us in San Leandro, with my mother. We had the house to ourselves most of the time, and a liquor store right down the street from us. I remember being so attracted to these twin sisters who were in my older brother's grade. They had paged me looking for some speed, which I had at the time. We took a little car ride, and they were so tweaked out. I think they offered to suck my dick or fuck me for drugs. I was still a virgin at the time. I played it off like it was okay, and that I just wanted money. If the girls were still normal, I would have loved to have them be my first. The Christian kid in me was frightened of what had happened to them, and I was seeing the harsh reality of what drugs can do to people.

We were not ready for what was to happen next. I remember waking up to the sound of an ambulance at my house. My middle brother was out the night before with one of his best friends, who was a secret enemy; the competition between them was too strong. My middle brother was partying with morning glories, a mescaline, two very strong hallucinogens. I have no idea where or how he found them, or how his friend came across them either. I have never even seen those drugs to this day or been offered them from any source.

My brother had taken too much and was 5150'd. Before I could get downstairs, he was in the back of the ambulance. Never ever was he the same again to this day. This hit me hard, and my cousins. They stayed away from drugs as kids. I felt lost and didn't know what to do. I stopped for a little while and watched to see what would happen. I had pretty good control over my limits. My older brother kept on being himself and was also pretty twisted from the loss of our brother. We were a bit relieved. My middle brother was bigger than both of us and was able to assert his dominance over us at any time. My mother was tired of taking us to school in Castro Valley, and I attended school in San Leandro.

Now this was for 10th grade. This school was right next to Oakland and had real gangs where the crips actually killed people. One person had died on the school grounds from a shooting.

With my understanding of life at the time, I realized I was still a Christian school kid with a little bit of worldly knowledge. I was in a white middle-class school district with wannabe gangsters. This was all mostly for show, and they copied the real and what they saw on TV and heard in the rap songs. I quickly removed my pride and ego from where I was to where I am. I knew I was in the real world now. I lost my strong brother, and the divide between me and my oldest brother was growing. I was alone. I needed to be smart. I found a guy who was similar to me, and we became best friends. We were part of a little clique called ASD. I needed friends, and they became my homies. We had a weight class at school that I was really happy to be part of. I loved lifting weights, and this was where you would find me most of the time.

I had this issue. My older brothers had me stealing these Playboy Penthouse magazines, and I was looking at these girls, and I was so frustrated, as I was still a virgin. I could have had some not-so-attractive girls to have sex with, but I had let my pride win. I wanted the perfect girl to be my first. She came across me in this new school. She was confident and beautiful. She was a ghetto white girl with attitude, and super light blonde hair. I've always had my choice of really hot girls. Ever since I learned how to talk to them, I felt in control. I am a mix of German/Latin. In my mind, I am a Californian. I fit more into the white category in life, but in reality, I am right in the middle. I don't speak Spanish, yet I still want to learn.

My dad worked for the United States government, and we were private school kids with polo shirts. Masked by music, drugs, and not being under strict parental rules anymore.

So, I had her come over to my house one weekend, and we got to hang out. She was definitely down to fuck. We had these new 64 ounces of beers that had just come out. I had already been buzzed on drinking before she got there. I was nervous as fuck.

I gave off this bad ass confident vibe walking through the halls at school, and she assumed I was like all these other guys who were born and raised in the hood. I was moonlighting in the hood. I realized she didn't care about my truths, and she just wanted to say she fucked me. I know that because right before we had protected sex, I had told her I was a virgin, and she laughed. She was like, 'Fuck, you don't have to lie to me, I don't care.'

I was shocked. I was giving her my soul, and she didn't want it. She wanted the bad ass guy I was pretending to be. They say fake it till you make it. I was learning from the hard knocks of life. The truth is, I fell in love with her and became stage 5. She wanted nothing to do with me after she figured out I really was a virgin. I felt like my soul was taken; the innocence of love was not an option for me. The girl I waited for was a cold-hearted snake that bit me, and the poison was strong. My heart was broken, shattered into millions of pieces.

I had no clue how to be or give her what she wanted. And this is the kind of girl I continue to love to this day.

Money, prestige, and power are what these girls want.

Walking past her in the hallways for the year to come was a nightmare. The girl I loved, I could see but could not please. No other girl was worth the time of day. I went to the gym, and before I knew it, the year was over. I did have other girlfriends; it just took time to move on. I remember going to the malls with my friends and meeting girls. I was the fearless one, always starting conversations and reading body language.

By this time, I had stopped selling weed after my brother did not come back to sanity, and after heartbreak, I realized it was time to pull my life together. I walked by a telephone pole that offered $200 or more a week selling newspaper subscriptions. I had an addiction to video games, and Mortal Kombat, Street Fighter 2 were my favorites. In order to fulfill my addiction, I got a job; my mother was tired of giving me money. This was one of the best days of my life. I learned how to talk to even more people, including random strangers. All the education of selling chocolate door to door, I used to sell newspapers door to door. We also used to sell outside of grocery stores. There was a guy named Mike who trained us. We sold the Daily Review, the Oakland Tribune, the Tri-Valley Herald, and the San Francisco Chronicle. The pitch was that I am trying to earn money for my college education, and would anyone like to help me earn some points? The way you help me is by letting me help you. Do you like to read current events? Do you use coupons? The newspapers have $50-100 worth of coupons in them, and all you have to do is subscribe to your favorite newspaper. It's only 14.99 for 3 months, etc. I was killing the game back then. I was a top seller, and I no longer had to deal with the bad effects of selling drugs. I had money for clothes and money for video games. I learned how to work for myself. I learned how to be said no to, and not get upset. I learned how to talk to people without getting them upset or letting them say no too fast to me.

My mother got a new job with Wells Fargo, and so we moved to Walnut Creek. I started school in Concord when we finally got our own apartment; it was walking distance to my new high school, about 3 blocks away. This was awesome. I was no longer in the Ghetto. I got to start my new school with a clean slate, no one knew me, and I was able to evolve a grow and use all my previous info to become successful.

My neighbor was a girl who fell in love with me. She was a really soft girl, and her name was Judy. We had an innocent love, although I was more her friend than her lover. I had the upper hand because I wasn't that attracted, but I needed the times we shared together to mend my heart and teach me what a good girl was and is. She had her sister and mother living with her, and they were very nice people. They followed the rules of life like most normal people. I still thought I was a good boy. Little did I know, I had changed on the inside, and what I attracted was the darker side of life. The knowledge of pain and suffering, nudity, drugs, and alcohol was all in my consciousness. None of this was on Judy's mind; she was baking cookies and working at an ice cream parlor, and she was a perfect girl with a big heart. I wanted the girls who were in the magazines. I wanted the 10s of the world. The girl every man dreams of. The ones who are not afraid of sex.

My junior year was slightly uneventful; I got fair grades and worked out with the football team, and I just went through the motions of life.

During the summer, my mom decided to get another job. This time, we would be moving across the Bay Area to Marin City. My mother took a job in Sausalito at a new Day Spa that was being built. I was able to get a job working with her as a spa assistant. This is where my life was really jaded. The poison of sex and drugs, and drinking would scare me for life. I was seventeen years young and my mother had me working for this woman who was a very high-end escort. She had received 250k to start this new day spa; she told me not to drink or smoke pot with her. This night I was to stay at her place and work in the morning for her at the spa. She was this blonde woman with fake tits and was so hot! That night we drank champagne a smoked pot. I was so attracted to her. I was unable to make a move on her, and as the night ended, I fell asleep on the couch warmed by the fire burning in the fireplace.

She asked me if I wanted to sleep in the bed downstairs. I was like, "I'm okay, I don't need, too." She sort of encouraged me to, so I was like fuck it, I will. When I opened the door, there was another woman already in bed. I shyly told her that I would go back upstairs and sleep on the couch. She was like, "It's okay, just sleep next to me. It's okay."

So being drunk and high, I was like, "Okay, I will."

Somehow, she started to come on to me, and we had sex.

She was many years older than me. She was an old woman, a nightmare. She may have been cute when she was younger, but she was not someone I ever wanted to be with. The feeling of sex was a drug, and I was told not to tell my mother; we woke up and went to work. This woman worked with us, and we would have sex at work during business hours. She would buy me clothes, and she bought me a watch. This would lead to an understanding of an addiction to the fact that people would take care of me. As time went on, my mother figured out what had happened; this woman was disrespecting her, and I feel so guilty for allowing all this to happen. When I finally told my mother the truth, we went to the police and I told them my story. Statutory rape was what had happened. I was taken advantage of and used. The police did nothing about it, and my mother did not have the ability to hire an attorney or find a way to make this woman pay for what she had done to me. This woman had a butterfly tattoo above her ass crack. She had the tramp stamp.

This destroyed or greatly damaged my relationship with my mother, and my father was already gone and unable to help just didn't participate in our lives anymore. This all happened right before I was to start my senior year at Mt Tamalpais in Marin. I had no idea the impact that this would have on my self-esteem. Not to mention being really poor in a very wealthy school. This school was so rich, they had a kid with convertible M3s pulling up to school. I was so poor that I worked at Ross, and all my clothes were from Ross. I had come back to see Judy one day, and everything that had happened in between the time had pushed us so far apart. That night, we got drunk off tequila and had sex for the first time. This temporarily fixed my soul from the stain of an older woman that was left behind on me. I had to go back to school, and Judy and I barely ever talked.

I never told her what had happened to me. I was again the new kid in a brand-new school. I was part of the football varsity team. I signed on as a kicker. I had a great soccer background, and they taught me how to kick field goals and punting. I remember this one time I woke up late to go to the football game and didn't get to eat breakfast. When I kicked off the game, I totally messed up the kickoff. It only went 15 yards, and the other team was able to start off the game with a great field advantage. They scored, and we scored, and I missed the extra point. The coach came over to me and asked, "What's wrong with you?"

I told him I was starving, I was so hungry. One of the cheerleaders was able to go buy me some nachos, and I devoured them. We had to punt the ball, and I kicked an amazing kick. We made the other team fumble, and we scored a touchdown. I made the extra point, and the kickoff to get the game going was amazing. We won that game, and on the way home, the whole bus was singing Nacho Nacho Man.

It was an incredible feeling. This school would teach me about the great divide between the wealthy and the poor. I was a second-class citizen, and I felt undatable because I was poor. I was angry because I had come from a middle-class family in private school, made it through the gangs and the drug selling, and pulled myself out of being raped and kept going. I was heartbroken and couldn't do anything about it. I didn't know how to make it.

I was lacking in being loved and was emotionally scarred. I joined a community outreach program in Marin City called Youth Taking Charge. I was the only non-black person in the group. This teacher of mine would be able to help me realize that if I tried to change my life, my life would change. When I was playing football, I was on the sidelines 95% of the game as a kicker. I had a huge heart and rooted for my team with the greatest passion. The cheerleaders noticed this, and when it was basketball season, they asked me to be a cheerleader. I came from the hard knocks school from before and knew no one could punk me for being a cheerleader, so I did. I took the chance. It was a very difficult thing to do. I knew that the year would be over and none of this would matter. I also knew that when I stand up to my fears, I learn a lesson a grow as a person. I wanted to be liked, and I always loved the cheerleaders. This was my chance to hang out with them. I didn't realize how different my life was compared to theirs. Coming from such privilege, they couldn't realize how much pain and suffering I was trying to mask.

I couldn't afford the uniform that they needed me to buy. I struggled to learn the dance moves, and honestly, I didn't really want to learn. It felt weird to me. I was wearing Ben Davis, carrying knives, and selling drugs—yet here I was, dancing in front of the whole school with all the varsity cheerleaders. They would have to come to my house a give me private lessons. I finally got it. We drove to LA to compete in the national competitions. I was able to meet amazing people from all over the country. I had a huge crush on this new girl, Nancy, who was so rich and smart she knew better and stayed away from me; this hurt a lot. I know I was tall, good-looking, talented, strong, poor, and brown. She never loved me.

I never knew what she felt about me, truthfully. During the final of the cheer competition, she was at the top of our pyramid, and she fell. It really hurt us in the points, and I'm sure the stress was intense. I was torn. I felt like she fell off her high horse of pride. She was lucky she wasn't hurt, that I remember. I'm sure it was embarrassing. Being embarrassed was a near-impossible thing for me; I had been stripped of all my hopes and dreams. I knew the odds were against me in all ways, and I could feel that at a young age. The worst possible things happened to me that I could have never dreamed; my parents splitting, my brothers turning on me, my mother being gone, and my innocence of sex stolen from me. I faced the biggest forms of shame, and nothing was worse than what had already happened to me. Later that year, my mother took me to a party she wanted to go to. She was drinking, and this guy tried to kiss her. It looks like she didn't want that kiss while she was intoxicated. She bit his lip, and it was bleeding. The word got through the party quickly, and I was like WTF. At the time, I didn't know it was her, and she came to me and said, "Let's go, we're leaving."

I realized it was her, and she was too drunk to drive. So, I took the keys in my hands without a license and drove her home. I told her I should drive because I don't need a license as much as she does. If I got caught, she could still drive to work. From Livermore to Pleasant Hill was 25 miles, and from Pleasant Hill back to Marin City was another 25 miles. I was able to take my mom to her boyfriend's house, and then I was off to Marin City. I was merging on the freeway, and on my blind side, a car was coming, and I crashed. The police came, and I was in jail for a DUI. I called the man who helped me from Marin City at Youth Taking Charge, and he was able to get me out of jail.

Life was really tough for me growing up. I had court to attend in the following months. No injuries happened in the car accident, insurance covered everything, and when the court came, I was really lucky; the criminal charges were dropped, and I only had to deal with the DMV. School was coming to an end. I was not sure if I was going to college. Neither of my parents had gone to college, and I was the first generation in this country. My mother was born in Mexico, my father left Pennsylvania, and was completely disconnected from his family when he moved to California. I had only met my father's parents when I was 1 year old, and it took 30 years in the future for me to fly back with my dad to see his mother one last time before she passed.

Moving Out of My Parents' House

High school ended, and I had to move back in with my father, who had been missing from my life for 5 years. We were disconnected, and it took some time to get used to life with him. He was always stable, paid all the bills, and went to work on time for 30 years straight at the same job.

I was 19 years old, and I found a job working for 24-Hour Fitness; I was an example of health and fitness. I was able to sell gym memberships at the rate of 20k a month. I had my first desk job and my first business cards. I was able to save money, work out, and learn to have a life outside of school. With my dad's help, I did my taxes, got a large tax return, and was able to buy my first car. My first car was a red Mazda RX7. It was about 5k, and I was able to pay cash for the car. I remember getting my license and feeling really good about life. I had a fresh new start.

I drew a picture of the car I wanted—or really liked. It had the sleek body of a sports car. Later in life, I realized that the car I drew was exactly the car I got. What I needed most in life now was a good relationship with a girl that I loved. On New Year's Eve of 2000, many people were afraid that all our computers would reset due to the Y2K bug, so a lot of the regular party people chose not to go out and celebrate that night. However, I still went out that night.

I met the girl who would become my first real relationship. At the time, I had a huge crush on Sarah Michelle Gellar from *Cruel Intentions*, and to me, this girl looked just like her. We got along really well. During one of our phone calls, I heard a baby in the background. I found out that she was a young mother at 22. On the other hand, I was 19 when I fell in love with her. Regardless, we spent about a year and a half together. She healed most of the pain, loneliness, and emptiness I had been feeling for years since I was 16. We were a match made right here on Earth.

We would go out dancing together in the city as we both liked to party. She drove a white Jetta, which I thought was so hot. She had that attitude of privilege, and she was very sexy and provocative. I loved the fact that she would sneak me into her parents' house at night while they were sleeping. We would make love and fall asleep in each other's arms, and when we woke up, her parents would be at work. We must have had sex everywhere in her parents' house. She was what I wanted and needed. We used to meet halfway to the city, park our cars, hook up in mine, then head downtown to party all night. We'd do lines of cocaine and sneak off to the private bathrooms in VIP and fuck. Sometimes, we didn't even bother—just went for it right there on the VIP couch. We didn't think anyone could really tell, and if they did, it didn't matter to us. We had sex on the dance floor one time, against the wall. Luckily, we never got caught or in trouble. I continued to work at 24-hour fitness and share life with my girl.

At the time, the internet was just beginning to emerge, and I advised my father to invest in a computer, which he subsequently did. He joined a Christian dating website, and just a few months later, he was selling his house to get married. This led me to find a new place to live. I was looking to live in an upper-middle-class neighborhood, and so I found a place in

Dublin. It was a four-bedroom place. I finally got freedom from all the family rules.

I shared the place with three other white guys and paid my share of the rent. I could finally have my girlfriend come stay with me, smoke weed in the house, put pictures of girls on my walls, come home as late as I wanted or not at all. This was the true separation I had needed so badly; I realized I no longer belonged in that family. I was a wild, wild child and had raised myself and made all my own decisions. The greatest thing I did for myself was visit a strip club and see my favorite girl. We went into VIP, and she danced for me. I still remember what she looked like dancing for me. The way she moved was so seductive. It was awesome and weirdly addictive no christian bible can ever make up for what this heaven is when she does what you want.

One day, that same dancing girl walked into my gym, and I couldn't help but think, wow! Nothing ever really happened. She was shocked that someone knew she was a dancer. It was just a one-time fling. However, it was a taste of the world outside my first love. Even with all the crazy fun sex with my girl, she had a baby, and I was incapable of settling into what that meant. The thought of someone calling me 'daddy,' that wasn't my baby, was a nightmare.

While I was working at 24-hour Fitness, one of the front desk guys became a friend of mine. I was making way more money than he was, but he had a second job that I did not know about. One day, he came to work with a wallet full of cash, and he proudly showed it off to me. All I could think was, *what the fuck?* How did you make all this money? He made me promise not to tell anyone, and I found out he was stripping at the place in San Francisco. He said his modeling agent told him he could make extra money doing this. He was taking classes at a place called *Lights. Camera. Action.* I wanted to be a model and an actor, so I signed up for the classes.

I also decided to lose my fear of being naked. I felt like I had lost my fear of crowds and what people thought of me as a cheerleader back in high school. So, if I ever wanted to be an actor, I would have to get rid of my stage fright. Plus, I had such respect for the girl I fell in love with at the strip club, I wanted that power over people. I wanted to learn the ways of a hustler. I loved anything sexual, and my sexual desires were cut loose from any Christian beliefs.

This strip club in San Francisco made me sign a contract, and I was able to dance and make money to burn. I would make money stripping, then go to the other strip clubs and give that money back to the very sexiest girls. It was a world of cocaine, heavy drinking, strange people, and girls who wanted to fuck, no questions asked. Since this was San Francisco, men were let into the strip club. Actually, it was for men, and women occasionally walked in for bachelorette parties. When they did, I was a fucking animal. It was a bring-your-own beer place, and when women came in, we had the fucking best times. After a while, I got fired from there for having too much fun with the girls and taking them on the stage; they said it was a potential hazard.

Growing up, I was lost, and my family was consumed by anger and pain. We were torn apart from each other in a lot of different ways. I was selling drugs shortly after I left Christian school. The pain of the older woman getting away with rape made me feel like I was worthless and had nothing else to lose. I could go to jail for selling drugs and be a drug dealer, or I could deal with what men want in business, and make money in San Francisco. If I were a drug dealer, I would eventually get caught and have to do time and deal with men in jail, or I could not deal drugs and deal with men in real life and have my freedom.

I joined *Lights. Camera. Action.* and the main guy running it was a real creep. He liked to blow his students; shortly after, his business was shut down, and the money I had invested in it was gone. I was still with my girl, even though she had a baby. I wanted to break up, and I tried a million times, but I always kept coming back to her. By this time in life, my older brother came out of the closet and was open about his attraction to men, and I had to deal with them at the strip club. So, for his birthday, I took him to San Francisco. It was gay pride, and I had all the confidence in the world. I was 20 years old, had a great body, and wanted to show my brother how to live life. Pride had a main stage where they had all these dancers, and I wanted to be on stage overlooking the crowd of 50 thousand people. I took my shirt off and wanted to get on stage, and they let me up. I danced my ass off and loved every second of the attention.

Later that day, a man approached me and offered me a job at his restaurant, where they had go-go dancers. This would mark the beginning of my education in fashion and luxury— dining at fancy spots all over the city, shopping at Gucci, Saks Fifth Avenue, and splurging on $1,200 Jean Paul Gaultier crocodile-print red velvet pants. Prada shoes and full outfits followed. All of this style and sophistication was taught to me by my girlfriend. She taught me how to seduce people and make them buy you anything you want. The trick was to *tease, don't please.*

I still wanted to be a model and actor, so I came across JRP in San Ramon. I made friends with the people who worked there, and the main guy was gay. He liked to rub lotion on his models before he took a Polaroid. He was a very wealthy man and was the devil in disguise. Due to my previous experiences, I overlooked his bull shit. I wanted to be famous so bad that I was ready to pursue any opportunity I found. People were discovered here, and I wanted to take classes and fly to New York to be discovered. I found a job working with them doing sales, and that helped pay my way to New York. I made it to a place called I.M.T.A. in NYC. I walked the runways and filmed my experience. Unfortunately, I didn't have any luck this time around. I stopped working for 24-Hour Fitness and got a job working for this high-end retail women's clothing store in Walnut Creek. This beautiful, blue-eyed cowgirl hired me. She was from Montana, and she was a size 0, full of energy, and so nice and straightforward and confident. We worked together for about three to four months during the holidays. We both were in a relationship we wanted out of, and we learned from each other. We both smoked pot one day after work. She came to my house because my roommate sold pot, and she needed to buy some. Therefore, we were able to smoke together. She kept me on the team after the Christmas season was over. I worked with her until April came upon us. We would close the store together, and we became close, talking about everything while the customers weren't in the store. I vividly remember her talking about her boyfriend not wanting to fuck her in the ass. I was like, *what the fuck?* I told her that if I was her boyfriend, I would love to fuck her in the ass. I kind of knew she was going to be the next love of my life.

That night, we went to my house and smoked and made love for the first time. We made plans to break up with our current relationships. My birthday came, and I woke up with my boss in Los Angeles for my 21st birthday. This was the only way to break up with my first love. It was sad that she called me on my birthday, and I was in LA. I couldn't break up the normal way; after all, she was my first love. I didn't know how to break up. We should have broken up when she had the abortion; this was the only time I had ever gotten a girl pregnant. She would not have had the baby even if I wanted to. I was not ready, and at 35 years of age, I still am not ready. I need to get my book sold and find another successful girl, and get married; that's when I will be ready to have kids.

I always wanted to live in LA. And now I do. Seven years after my 21st birthday, I moved to LA for the first time. When we came back to the Bay Area, things got complicated at work. Everything was fine between us; it was the corporation that we worked for that had a problem. They started to give me fewer and fewer hours until I was no longer working there, and they basically forced my girlfriend to quit her job. Her mother was not happy about this; she looked at me as an undereducated man, a subordinate to her daughter. Her mother pulled some strings at her old job, and my girl was working for the bank in Walnut Creek. I took this matter to the Fair Employment and

Housing, a government agency that listened to my case and helped me fight back against this huge corporation. This was a big personal victory for me. I had done nothing wrong. I was only following my heart. I couldn't afford my own attorney, and this agency forced them to pay me for the lost wages.

I wasn't selfish with the amount of money I asked for; I was scared of meeting with their attorney. She intimidated me, made me feel like I was wrong for asking for this money, and I had no experience negotiating. My mother and father would not have been able to help me; this was where being poor and humble really hurt me. However, this wouldn't be the last time I needed to use this agency to fight against big corporations. I got a job working for Best Buy selling cell phones, Palm Pilots, and GPS systems. We decided to move in together, and this was the first time I had ever lived with a girlfriend. It was incredible. This was true love, this was young love. On our very first night in our new place in Pleasant Hill, we decided to take ecstasy and really create an elevated experience. We made love for hours and looked into each other's eyes so deeply that I could see her soul. We stepped outside to smoke a cigarette, both of us completely naked, wrapped in nothing but a blanket to keep warm. The sliding glass door we closed had a loose lock, and when we closed the door, the lock fell down and locked us out. We decided I would take the blanket and knock on the manager's door, and get the key to let us in. Living with her, I was lifted from my pain and suffering as a child. Love with one girl is enough for me to be the happiest man alive. Its just keeping that one girl happy is the secret to life.

I was working and living on my own. My past slipped away, and I became something I learned to forget about. I should have been in college, but I was living life and experiencing the bliss of what love should be. My mother and father had no part in my life. I was alone; it was just me and my girlfriend. I couldn't be happier. We got to decorate our loft-style apartment, which had a staircase leading up to our bedroom. The space was completely open, with no closed doors, so she could give me all her attention. This is what I needed most out of life: the love we got to share together. She introduced me to country music, and when I was with her, I could listen to it and appreciate it. She would smoke about a 1/8 of weed a week. We always could smoke, and it sort of became an issue later on in the relationship. I couldn't afford to keep on paying for the weed. She made more money than I did.

I remember some of the simple mistakes I made in the relationship. She would ask me to go get her something from the fridge, and I was tired of getting up and getting her things. Most of the time, I was either lazy or stoned. Now, if my girl asked me to get her something, I would always get it for her. I would never let a simple little task prevent us from having the peace we should have. We went to a town fair one day and purchased a little dwarf bunny. We made a little house for our bunny, and it was the cutest little gray bunny; it was softer than a chinchilla.

My girl decided to quit the bank job she had and started to work for a company called Outback Steakhouse; this was a mixed blessing. She would bring home steak and Alaskan king crab legs and all sorts of amazing food. The people at her work, including her boss's would hit on her, and she had so many men after her. She was a 100 lbs, blue-eyed blonde girl with 34C natural breasts. She was full of positive energy, and we made love every day. One day, we had sex 8 times, and I learned that I had such a large appetite for sex. We did have that anal sex we spoke of at work. I remember her letting me in, and she loved it so much. She was moving so fast she took my whole weight on her back. I was off the earth. I was completely in her, and it felt so good. She had the biggest competition with her best friend, and they competed for everything.

I love film, and we made home videos. When we broke up, it was not a good idea to keep watching these videos; they made me miss her more and reopened the emotional connection I had to her. She kept looking for better and better work while we were together. She was offered a job in San Francisco at another clothing store like the one where we both worked. When we met, she wanted to be a clothing designer, and she made me a pair of leather jeans that I still have to this day. She took the job in San Francisco on Union Street and moved to the city. When she finally moved, and the loft was all mine, I woke up every morning, and she was not there. I would cry from the deepest depths of my heart. Any time I listened to country music, I would begin to tear up. She found an investor who was attracted to her; he lived in Pacific Heights, and he gave her the money she needed to create 20 items of clothes. She wanted me to fly to Washington, D.C., for her first fashion show. I had found a job working for CompUSA in San Francisco on Market Street. Soon it would be time for me to move to the city. I had taken pictures of her fashion show and had them on my SD card in my Palm Pilot. I used to show people how cool it was to take pictures and view them on these devices. It moved merchandise, and one day the memory cared was stolen, and the pictures were gone before I could save them, and that's when we really broke up.

San Francisco

I packed up all my stuff into a truck and moved to San Francisco in 2002. I moved to Natoma on 11th Street in the neighborhood called Soma. This is where I really began to live a crazy lifestyle. This is where I finally had a female roommate whom I did not have sex with. She was my first platonic friendship as a young adult. We lived together, and that saved me from needing the feeling of having a girlfriend for the most part. Just being in the company of a cool girl as a friend was a really cool feeling. When we became really close friends, she would tell me her stories. One day, she asked me if I knew who Ron Jermey was. I told her I didn't. then she proceeded to say that she had gone to his hotel room at the Clift hotel and sucked his cock. I was like, 'Wow! Good for you.' She had a Latin boyfriend who would come along every once in a while. She loved him the most. He was an artist and a drunk. I remember seeing him drink a whole half pint of vodka in one sip. That was a real alcoholic to me, besides my mom's second husband.

He was really cool and we had a great friendship, but I realized she had lovers on the side and he was her man. If he pulled his shit together, she would have just been with him. He used to be a bouncer at a club, and I'm sure they met there and had that whole relationship where he gets her in the club, she sucks his dick, and he gets her free drinks and all her friends in. I started living with her and had a real job working for CompUSA, and now I was an assistant sales manager. I had done really well working with the public and getting sales and the extended service plans. I love technology. It is one of my biggest passions in life. I love to play with new technologies and learn them; they come to me very quickly. I had started to be a consultant for 50$ an hour, teaching people how to set up their new technology. I called it, "In the Palm of Your Hand." I wish I had more college education; I would have still had this company and made millions of dollars with all the legal paperwork. I was thankful people would let me work for them on the side. I always loved helping people find the truth or teaching them the way to make something work. The months kept on coming, and I was promoted again to the front-end manager. I was able to have keys to the store, and I was able to hire and fire staff. I was in charge of all the money and credit cards and sales, and returns for the whole store.

One day, I was upstairs working, doing returns, and this couple walked in. They were both very tall and attractive; my guess was that they were models at one point in their lives. So, I took care of them, overlooking a late return, and asked them what they did for a living. They told me they had their own modeling agency in San Francisco. I took a business card and kept in contact with them. I helped them scout girls in SF for their agency, which gave me a bit of power and reason for really hot girls to be nice to me. This was training for how things worked in L.A. I would go out at night and go to the clubs and really cherry-pick girls for this company. It was lots of fun. They had a big fashion show that was coming up. I was helping them prepare; they had a great flat in Pacific Heights overlooking the Golden Gate Bridge with access to the top floor. We had stayed out all night doing lines of blow, and they needed me to stay and help the very next morning, and I hadn't slept yet. At the same time, CompUSA was doing inventory, and I had scheduled myself off, but they called me in.

I had a choice to make, and this choice would change my life forever. Either go to work and count computers at 7 am and it was already 3 am, or stay in bed with these 3 models and work for a talent agency. The talent agency never really paid me much. Nobody wants a normal job. We would all love to make money for traveling. The drugs and the girls, and the fame were all I ever wanted in life at the time. I gave in to every feeling of pleasure I came across, and losing my normal job didn't really affect me too much. Telling my roommate was the hardest part. I still had ways to make money; I got my job back dancing as a stripper. The goal here was to get private shows. Private shows would make you a solid amount of cash that would last a few days and pay rent. You have to learn how to silence your conscious, that little voice that's telling you not to do this; that voice will prevent you from living your dreams.

I had so much time on my hands now, always working at night and going out to the clubs and meeting people. I remember getting a bag of cocaine and spelling my name in the coke and doing the whole thing at one time when I was at home. I was so high—living in a fantasy, detached from reality, even though everything was actually happening. I couldn't feel the truth, and as long as no one knew what I was doing, it felt like it wasn't real. Little did I know my own self-consciousness was aware that all these things really did happen to me, even though I thought highly of myself when the cameras were around for photo shoots. My self-esteem wasn't where it should have been. Smiling just to smile wasn't real; I wasn't really happy. I would go to the strip clubs and meet girls who liked that I was a model; they wanted to be where I was, and loved my portfolios; they would like to come to the parties with me and have carefree sex with me for free. I do take pride in never having paid for the girls I slept with, even though they charged people for dances. My mindset was that rich men were paying these women for fake love, while I got their bodies for free, so in my mind, I was saving money and felt superior to the men who had to pay for them.

I met this guy who was a straight hustler from Russia. He was dressed in DIOR and had a 20k HERMES purse. He taught me some things in life. The most important thing he did was introduce me to my new hairstylist. I will call him ON. We became friends, and he let me work for him part-time at his salon. He introduced me to a modeling agency that was willing to take on a new model. I shot with their photographers and built a real portfolio. Many months went by without me booking any work. They decided to let me go, and I played a funny prank on them. I immediately signed with another agency and started to book my first modeling jobs. I was on MTV, I shot for AAA, and worked for the FORD car company. This place, called 'Show Girls' at the time, was my favorite Thursday night hangout before going to the Mark Hopkins hotel parties. I was hanging out with my usual crowd of girls I'd already slept with, when along came this magical creature, like something out of a dream. She was walking over to me to see why these other girls were swarming. She was the ultimate fantasy; her face was more golden than the famous King Tut we all know. A body that was 98 lbs with double D's, green eyes, blonde hair, and a rock star personality.

I completely ignored her and acted like she wasn't there till she made her move, and I struck like a viper; I stole her attention. I belittled her knowledge to get the upper hand. I had VIP parties in multi-million dollar venues with famous people. She was star-struck, and I was a model with an agent, which is one level above a stripper. I took her number, which I still have memorized to this day. It took us about a month to really hang out for the first time outside the club. I had to move to 26th and Geary—it felt so far from downtown. My friendship with my roommate had changed, and she needed to leave. She realized the city had its grip on me, and it was time for her to move on. She knew I had no real job anymore, and I was out all night and sleeping all day, you could see it on my face, I'm sure, I probably told her.

I had a couple of regulars that I saw. One was in Tiburon, and this was fairly secure; we would fly to Hawaii, and no sex was required. I never sold any kind of sex to anyone. That was crossing the line to me; if I had, I would have really been over the edge. I had a job being a go-go dancer as well. I had friends who worked at restaurants and would give me free lunches and dinners. I was a middleman for jobs that would provide profit, and I built a network of minor hustles. My fear of jail was too high. I could not ever get into deep enough to anything. I was still a kid at heart, and my credit cards got maxed out. I was 8k in debt at this point in life. Like all young people, we change are phone numbers, we ignore the calls, and believe it will all go away, and if not, we just kill ourselves. The exterior was rich with labels, and the interior was becoming dark like dark matter, like emptiness, a void of matter in outer space. I was an actor; this is the beginning of the act. We pretend we lie to ourselves and we make you believe what we want, assuming you are doing the same thing.

My past two relationships would be nothing like this new one about to form. So, the new stripper and I met at my house in the Richmond district. She was coming from San Rafael in Marin County, and my hair was in an afro. I had long hair, and it just did that. I wanted to surprise her; I thought it looked good. I sent my roommate down to let her in; he nearly had a heart attack. He was like, "Why did you not tell me how beautiful she is?"

I told him that I didn't think I had to warn him about her fire. I was broke, and so I was like, "Let's go to the beach."

This was the best thing I could have done. Everyone else was like, "Let me take you to a fancy place." She was from Michigan—a small-town girl, who likes a walk along the beach at sunset. She let me give her a piggyback ride. Our next date was to the top of the Mark Hopkins hotel; she took a girlfriend with her to keep her safe. We overlooked the entire city, and my friends looked at me like, *How the hell does Jason get these incredible girls?* I was living the dream—on cloud nine. I lived for moments like this.

At the end of the night, I was asking if she wanted to come home with me or to her girls' place. The girls looked at each other, and she decided to come with me. The sex was incredible. She was the type of girl you couldn't keep your hands off of. Everything about her says, 'Fuck me.' sex is written in everything she does. She was a goddess of beauty and the body of a dream. She would understand me being a stripper, and I did not have to hide my truth from her, as she did not have to hide her truth from me. This was my dream girl: openness and reality. Nothing to hide. I gave her the insight into men and how to manipulate them. I thought she was a Vegas girl, and she was only 19 when I met her. In fact, I helped her become a Vegas girl. I was the premier form of advice on how to hustle. I have a gift of knowing people. I can read all sorts of body language and tones of voice, and I know what questions to ask to penetrate your soul. I can see why your relationship is failing, and I can diagnose problems. I can set you free from yourself.

This is my vice. I have advice, I have knowledge, and one day I will have a solid business on rehabilitating people to help them achieve their goals. I am a loving, caring person, and if I take you under my wing, I want loyalty and love. Otherwise, pay me for my time and efforts. As a hair stylist now, I get to share support and watch my clients thrive in L.A. We were going to become famous in San Francisco's nightlife! Everyone would know who I was and who my girl was. We were always invited and on the list for all the parties. We made money and partied. I gave her some rules to follow, and one of those rules was never to let anyone you met at your strip club into your house. She met this guy who was twice her age and from Vegas. He faked his accent, and she fell for it all. I woke up in the middle of the night at 4 am and called her. She didn't answer. He was in her house. He promised to make her a famous singer and pay for her college, and she was sold. I was willing to let her go because I could not convince her he was a liar. I could tell he was selling her a dream he would never come through on. I wouldn't be able to stop her, so as the saying goes, 'If you love someone, let her go; if she comes back to you, it was meant to be.' I didn't want to be the one who stopped her from living her dreams. If I could not provide her with her future success, I would let her go and make it come true on her own.

This was a character trait of love, something a normal man would not have. The following days would be dark for me; I would lose my way in life. I worked part-time for this clothing company during the holidays. It was in Union Square and the name rhymes with Lil Bitch. This company could have made me a famous model/actor, yet they had racist ways. I was watched by an all-white management when I could have been a manager myself. My experience at CompUSA was far superior to what these kids had to do, and my body was in great shape—I should have been chosen. The funny thing was, I felt attractive, and when my modeling agency got me work, I felt even more attractive and marketable. When this company hired me, I felt like I was let into a secret society. This was the pinnacle of natural beauty. I felt like here it is, this is how I will become famous and be able to have a microphone to speak to the world and share my truths with everyone. I went to the cattle call audition for the new catalog and waited and waited to hear, and nothing ever came of it. I felt a sense of discrimination. I wanted to fight back and say this wasn't fair. I had no proof or outlet to voice my opinion.

Mr. BIG

Now, even though I was an entertainer for women and men, I was still homophobic at this point in my life. That is where alcohol came into play, dancing in the Castro at night, going to auditions in the daytime, and working weekends for this clothing company, with a broken heart. I felt like women made more money than me, and in both of these industries, they do; strippers and modeling girls make way more money. I always envied women because they are pursued and taken care of, and loved; men do all the work and provide. I felt like the world had fucked me and I would never be able to find a way to get an education or be loved. I always felt that my girl would leave me for a man with more money.

All she had to do was spread her legs open, and men would throw money at her; she would come home with two to four grand a night as a showgirl. This was insane money. If I were making that kind of money, I would have invested in real estate and started a legit business. Life was so unfair, and I had no way out. I wanted to rob a bank. I wanted my girlfriend back. One day, while dancing in the Castro, I was found by a banker who took a liking to me. I knew immediately because I found a $20 bill had been put into my YSL swimsuit. I received a business card that said 'President' on it; this was my new best friend. 'Call me,' it said, as I was fading away into the depths of lights, party people, drugs, nightlife, raves. All my money was gone. Rent was due the next day, and I couldn't sleep because of the cocaine. The sun was coming up, and I was feeling so stressed out. I saw that card and knew what it meant. It was another one of those, but so much better. I called to let everyone know I was very lucky to meet this person; my life was saved.

I would have moved back home or become homeless. I was at rock bottom in life. The man I am today would not be who he is without this. This friendship tested all of my religious beliefs and made me question everything I knew about life. I told him my situation, and he offered to let me live with him. I had no other choice. I lived at his beautiful house for one week before we found my new place in Lower Pac Heights. Again, I was moving into another gay man's house. This time it was different because he liked me, but he had no ability to cross that line. He didn't meet me at the clubs; this was platonic. Fred was an incredible house guest; he took care of me, made dinner for me, and was like an uncle who loved me. I made him happy just by being nice and by being in his life. I had 3 bedrooms for $700 with a 13-foot ceiling and French doors. All of this was graciously financed by Mr. Big. My gift to Mr. Big was still dancing and showing off my body. I was an escort, in my mind, and in his mind, I was his boyfriend whom he would try a break in. He did not realize how strong I was. I felt saved. I had money and a new place to live closer to the city.

I was going to the fanciest restaurants in all of San Francisco, and 3 times a week, we would go out. Dinners cost around 500$ every night we went out. The 5th floor was one of my favorite places. I got a gym membership to the sports club LA This is where I would join the soccer league and meet fun adults who made fortunes living life the right way. They all had college educations and normal jobs, and they were living like kings. I felt like a pretty woman. I had no other way to describe it. I started to go to places like HRC, and that is when I had my first tuxedo purchased for me. This was something my father was supposed to be doing for me. My dad was gone and had no way of shaping me into a man. At the time, I saw him as a zero.

Now, the HRC (Human Rights Campaign) had a table up front. I heard stories of how men suffered the inequalities of life because of their sexual orientation. This touched my heart. I greatly felt the pressure of life and felt belittled. I knew I was not measuring up to anyone's standards of life. I was a BIG LOSER. I had sold my soul. I chose to stay in bed with the models and do cocaine instead of count computers. My second girlfriend's mother made me feel like, without a college education, I would always be a loser, and why was her daughter with me? Now, why was I at the HRC? Because I am a fighter. I stand up to anyone who treats me unfairly. I have a huge heart, and I will fight for all my brothers and sisters to have equality in the United States of America. I will take down the establishment and rebuild it with equality for all. I will make right what is wrong and make fair what is unfair. I heard stories that changed my life, and I could no longer believe that being gay was a sin. Forget religion—and anyone who believed that God didn't want men to be with men or women to be with women was just blindly following what the Bible says.

You have no experience with the truth of life if you didn't know that we are all here to help one another live the life we would want to live ourselves. I was being taught what it's like to be gay. I went to LGBT fundraisers and heard more heartbreaking stories. In all reality, these people are some of the nicest people in the world. The straight world is very tough. It is full of wannabe Donald Trump's egotistical fools, a supremacist. On June 28th, 2015, I went to the Abbey in LA to celebrate that everyone can be married to anyone, the new love of my life. My own father turned his back on me and did not care if I went to college or not. He only wanted me to follow his rules and live life like him. He did not do what it took to keep my family together. My brothers have lost their way in life and are in a prison of their own making. Mr. Big did take me to these places as I was learning about life. I did not know if he was a nice person. I went along for the ride because I had no other choice. I saw this as a job, but I wasn't convinced, and I remained true to myself and my feelings.

I don't like masculinity; I prefer the feminine. I appreciate soft, cool women with their cold hands on my warm chest. I missed my girl for close to a year; we didn't speak. I continued a blessed life, without rules, and the party kept on going for me; I still had all my connections, and I had the best place in the city to live. Soon, I would have a closet full of new clothes, a business suit, and DKNY bedding; I had a Platinum American Express to shop at bae. I took trips to New York and bought Versace and a Dior. We spent 10k in NYC on me. I got diamonds at Boots, and we partied all night at the clubs. We went to female strip clubs and drank expensive champagne. I tried to make him straight, and he tried to make me gay. When we came back, I was able to get a new BMW, and I was on cloud nine in life. I had all the blessings of someone who had worked a 9-5 and gone to a prestigious college. I wanted a tattoo to get me over my last relationship; this would be my first tattoo ever. I was in the depths of so much emotional pain;

I wanted to drive a stake through my heart. Love is the most important thing to me in this world, always has been, and always will be. I hated that she could just spread her legs and men would drop to their knees and beg for her. I wanted a power similar to this. I was part of a modeling agency and couldn't have tattoos on my arms. I wanted to get something that would prove how tough I am; I wanted something jaw-dropping and unforgettable.

I wanted something no one else had; I came to the conclusion that only a star tattoo on my balls would prove this! The pain of this tattoo would overcome the pain in my heart, and it did; this became the reality. I chose a blue star because the blue star is the hottest and brightest star in the universe. I came to help men become better to their women, and for that to happen, they must understand how women feel. I am an adventurous soul, and I will succeed in life by all means. I always win. I enrolled in the Academy of Art College in San Francisco; I was about 26 years old when I finally went to college. I decided I wanted to make Super Bowl commercials, and I was fully supported for this decision. Again, I wish this were something my mother and father wanted for me. They did not or could not pay for this. I will always be in disbelief that this was the way I was to attend college by dancing in the city. I was way past feeling any shame. I had hit rock bottom in the past, and I only felt lucky to go to school. I got a new MacBook computer and a new camera to build my future as a student and a professional. I knew that I could always find the best feature of any product and bring it to light in a wonderful and creative way. The Academy of Art School costs $30,000 for one year, which I am still paying off. The debt compiles interest, and it has not been a fun weight to carry around all these years.

The good news is that I was able to learn how to use Photoshop and Illustrator; I took marketing classes, which taught me some techniques companies use to track their customers. I was able to learn how to paint in Acrylic, and I still love to paint. This college would allow me to learn how to use Final Cut Pro later on in life and make films. One day, my ex-girlfriend's best friend called me and was like, 'Hey, I am in the city. Can you show me around?'

This was the girl I lived with in Pleasant Hill—the one I told you about with that whole competition thing. She wanted to sleep with me, and I saw it. I gave her the chance, and it was incredible. I felt vindicated. Also, around this time, a lawsuit had emerged about the clothing store I had worked for in SF that rhymed with "zombie & bitch." I took that class-action lawsuit and went to the Fair Employment Housing and found a way to make them swallow their pride. This racism has to stop! I fought with everything I had in my soul, and we won on my birthday, in April. I personally showed up at the courthouse in SF to watch the outcome as they settled.

I was so frustrated by the looks of the attorneys who defended these cowards; I was on fire, hotter than the sun, wanting to give them a tan that would burn like Bernie Sanders. I had victory after victory, and I was on top of the world. That is when my girl came back to me. She called crying, saying her guy was cheating on her, and he lied about the singing lessons, and she was not famous or ever going to be for singing. He was corrupt, and she was done. She had moved in with him, and she needed my help to move her out of his house. he was coming home in a couple of hours. So, I drove over in my BMW, which she was very impressed with.

I helped her move the heavy TV and all of her belongings. She was living in a dump. It was nothing like I thought she had. She lived seven blocks from me on a parallel street, the whole time. I had so many mixed feelings about her at the time. I missed her, loved her so much, and I needed to know she would be mine again; that's all I wanted. After moving, we decided to meet for brunch, and she looked like a porn star when I saw her again, all dressed up. She had a boob job and they were no longer sagging. She was still the same girl I fell in love with. On Memorial Day, we made our relationship solid by getting her first tattoo. I helped her choose a heart that she put on her right cheek. I got the idea from Jenna Jamison, who had a broken heart on her left cheek, and I wanted my girl to have a solid heart.

I wanted her to be a centerfold playmate, so she wouldn't have to be a stripper anymore. I took pictures of her and we sent them in to Playboy. She moved into her own apartment near downtown. It was on the 12th floor; we had a cool view. She now had a new friend with her: a little poodle she named Baby. The balance between these two connections in life was a challenge to keep in line. One was jealous of the other, and they had two very different places in my life. One made room for the other to exist. Life was back to a place where I hit peaks; my girl was able to put $20,000 down on a new Mercedes C-Class, and we were two peas in a pod, enjoying a fancy lifestyle. We were both taken care of by the city in unconventional ways.

We had a good 6 months of pure happiness. My girl was getting into trouble at the club she worked at; she was caught with her panties down in VIP. She was fired and needed to go to Vegas for work. That night, I got way too drunk and drove home. I went through a light right as it turned green, and it was too fast. Another car was going through a red light, and we collided. I wanted to ditch, but I stayed; I was taken to jail. I was booked for a DUI. This one would stick and cause a strain on our relationship.

Mr. Big came to bail me out, and I was in jail for a few days. I refused to eat the food, and I was let into the general population for a few hours after moving from room to room for a few days. When I got out, I ran. I hated being locked up; all my privileges were taken from me, and it was a horrible feeling. I know that if my girl weren't in Vegas, I would not have drunk as much as I did, and I blamed her for being the reason this happened to me; she wasn't there to bail me out, nor was she there when I got out. Losing my car, my ability to drive, was a huge sadness for me. My girl was happy to pick me up a drive us around for a few months, and I was taking the bus again. I had classes to take for 18 months, and I had 180 days of street cleaning to do. We experienced a few more stressful events. I had a family trip to Mexico, and I had to leave the day after her baby dog passed away in a tragic car accident. This was heartbreaking, and she was probably learning to pull her heart away from me. We had a mutual friend whom I told not to trust the girl, and the girl was dating my close male friend. We would often go out as couples, which was a rage. The time came when she broke up with my friend, and she wanted my girl to break up with me. The girls wanted to take over the world, stripping for men, traveling back and forth to Vegas. The girls had it played out for them; men will pay top dollar for either of these girls. My girl's birthday was in September, and we celebrated her real 21st birthday in the Castro, where I was her prize. We had made plans to move to LA together, and after a few more fights, we split up. The girl I told her not to trust stole a lot of money from her, and she was pretty pissed about it. My girlfriend moved to LA before I did, and I had to complete 90 more days of community service before I could join her in LA. These 90 days of Street labor really brought me back to my humble beginnings. I was again empty and lost, with only my hopes and dreams to keep me alive. I did the 90 days straight. I packed up my bags and had a girl I met when I was visiting from LA drive my truck to LA.

The City of Lost Angels Round #1

I was now living off Sunset Blvd and Detroit. I had about 5k to my name, and I was a roommate to a 60-year-old straight guy who barely ever left his house; it was like living with a grandpa I never had. I had a large room with a separate entrance for only $700 a month. I lived just a few blocks from Hollywood. I thought I chose a central location to the nightlife scene, and my goal was to find an acting agent and get myself on TV as soon as possible. I became my own agent. I was in LA, casting and submitting myself to as many jobs as possible. I didn't have a normal job that would pay my bills. During my first week in LA, I partied a lot and spent about $500 on drinks. The hangovers weren't fun, and it took time to adjust to the new dry air. I still didn't have my license to drive cars, and this was before Uber existed, so I was taking the bus everywhere, and I would have to print out paper directions on MapQuest from location to location.

I believe the most auditions I had in one day were six, and I made it to them all. It was such an exhausting way to experience LA for the first time. I was living with a dream in my mind, and having no way to be taught how to make it in reality. I turned to reality TV. I think my first real job was on Playboy's reality show *Foursome*. It's a dating show that aired exclusively on the Playboy Network, featuring two girls and two guys spending 24 hours together in a mansion. I thought this was going to be pretty cool. I was still heartbroken from my breakup with my last girlfriend, and my standards were pretty high. That didn't go over well on the TV show, not to mention I wasn't drinking at the time, due to a disastrous New

Year's in LA where I ended up in North Hollywood Jail. I was robbed that night of three diamond earrings and my Dior watch, which cost $5,000.

So, the Playboy job only paid $500 to be on this show; I had no idea what its viewer count was; I just liked the name Playboy and assumed that the girls on the show would be Playmates. One of the girls was covered in tattoos and had done porn. We were in a mansion in the Hollywood Hills, overlooking the valley. To me, she looked a bit trashy—I was expecting someone more like a natural beauty, like Miss April. The other girl was from a Midwestern state, maybe Kentucky or somewhere like that. Neither girl was my type, and the guy was some skinny white guy who didn't mind having sex on camera because he had shot porn as well. So that guy and girl sort of connected right off, and I was left with the country girl, who wasn't anything like my ex-girlfriend. I was still so in love with my ex-girlfriend, and the thought of other girls took some time to get used to. So, the show starts by filming us walking in one by one and meeting and greeting. Then, we have our first challenge. They gave us army-type clothes and sweet icing to place on each other's bodies, and they had hired a really hot girl to come host this event. I was much more attracted to the new host they had brought us; she was telling me what to do with the other girls, and I wasn't having it. Even though she wasn't officially part of the game, I was still willing to lick icing off her body. We were having fun, and the show was off to a lively start.

This would have been a really fun show had I been attracted to any of the girls they set me up with. Also, if I didn't care about being sexual on camera, I could have just enjoyed the company; it was just one day, one show. I still had hopes and dreams of becoming a legit star, and being nude was going to degrade the quality of my character. As the show went on, they had prepared 2 limos to take us to a surprise location. Little did I know we were heading to a sex dungeon for S & M type bondage play. What a surprise indeed! I had never experienced such a mix of pleasure and pain before. I wanted this show to be fun; I really did. I can easily become defensive and put up walls that turn people against me. They asked me to put my arms up, and they locked me in a wooden device that had my neck and arms restrained. I was stuck there watching as one of the girls was bound to a table and they forced her to orgasm with Good Vibrations.

I was intrigued by her willingness, and I soon let myself out of the restraints by opening the lock. I was fighting the show; I wanted to have some control and be able to choose my destiny, and the more I fought, the more it backfired, turning my cast members against me. I remember opening up a little more after witnessing her have multiple orgasms in the same room as all of us, which opened up some playful nature. I realize people can understand that this is not an easy position to be in. I was happier not having any connection to either of the girls, and the other guy was able to have both girls. After we left the sex dungeon, we returned to the mansion, where a candlelit, side-by-side bathtub was waiting for us. The men were supposed to get in while the women fed us grapes and strawberries. It was all pretty nice. The water was too hot for anyone to get in; it was a funny mishap. They had to put ice in it to make the water cooler. Once this scene was done, we all went downstairs to the shower place and took a group shower and bath. By this time, the guy and girl started to have sex in front of us, and I wasn't willing to have sex or even kiss the other girl. So, I excused myself and fell asleep upstairs.

The whole experience totally let me down, although it was kind of exciting. I felt tricked and misled. My fantasy was much greater than reality. I'm fairly certain that this all came across on camera; I've never actually seen the footage of the show. I felt used, and I felt like the casting director chose people who did not fit in with my standards, and I had no control over who my partners were, which made me sad. I like that so many other people are willing to risk everything for a chance at fame and money. We want to be respected and recognized and treated like stars. We want to live lives that are not basic and redundant; we want to be able to travel the world and feel alive and welcomed by our peers without racial or monetary divides. The next thing we were able to do was become an extra for the movie Star Trek. We used to watch this show as kids, so being able to wear the uniform as part of a major motion picture was exciting, and receiving my first SAG voucher was thrilling. My mom and dad were proud of me, and my older brother was too; it was the first time walking onto a major studio to be part of the movie. I was excited to be part of a real production and felt like I was heading in the right direction, finally.

I continued to submit myself to small films on LA casting. I was able to book the lead role in a Japanese student film. I finally attended an audition without worrying about landing the role; I just went all out with the script. Fortunately, the character was meant to be upset, and I can convincingly portray anger. This movie was about a son and his father; the father was an alcoholic, and the son was raised by his mother. The boy was missing his father and never really knew him. One day, the father returned home to see his son, and his son was now 17. He yelled at his father, and as the son stormed off, he got hit by a car. This film was about 8 minutes long, and I felt like I now had a reel I could show an agent and get picked up by CAA. I was dreaming big. I needed more classes and a connection to an agency. Little did I know it's not that easy for someone like me. I had a much longer wait ahead of me. At the time, I didn't know it, so ignorance is bliss, and I kept on going.

My older brother wanted to move to LA, and my mother supported his move at the time. So, I got to upgrade my living situation with a move into a one-bedroom apartment right behind the Laugh Factory; it was $ 1350 a month. My brother moved into my old apartment. My older brother and I never really got along well; we would always try, and always end up fighting in the end. Sooner or later, I just gave up ever trying to be friends. I just accepted the fact that we would always be different, and it would never be like when we were kids. After I moved into my new apartment, I remember that this girl I used to work with in Walnut Creek, who was on an MTV reality show, lived in my apartment complex. We said 'Hi' to each other a few times. She was truly beautiful and probably had sugar daddies; she didn't show me much attention, although she was nice. Making friends with attractive women in LA can be challenging because every guy around gets jealous if she shows you any attention. People automatically assume you're either sleeping together or that one of you is trying to.

In the month of February, it was my mother's birthday, and also that year, the Super Bowl was being played right around the same time. I remember my mother was coming down to visit, and I was still very much wounded from my breakup with the girl I loved from San Francisco. She called me that day, crying; she was having a fight with her boyfriend at the time. He was being abusive, and she was making money dancing for the Rock Star drink guy and his girlfriend. He took her cell phone and read it, and then she chased after him. He pushed her to the floor and threw her phone at the ground, shattering it into pieces. So here was my chance to have my love back. This was very exciting to me. She gave me her address, which was only seven blocks from my apartment. We had moved to the same neighborhood and didn't even know it. So, I got ready and took a cab over to her house, and there she was, my angel, my love, everything I ever wanted in life. I knew that she needed me that night to help her. I asked her to call the police and report his violence, but she was unwilling to do so. I wanted her to cut the relationship off and start a new one with me. I had come to her rescue and put up a fight.

I had to realize that I came from a very strict father who would not tolerate such abuse, and she came from a place where calling the police was the very last resort, not the first. So, as we spoke, the night continued, and somehow, we called him or he called, and I was there to back her up. It turns out he was drunk, sleeping in his car right outside her house. We started talking trash about each other, and before we knew it, we were about to fight. I went downstairs and was talking to him through the glass door, and I thought he was locked out of the building. Little did I know he had the password to open the door. As I pointed my finger at him, telling him he was going to jail, he decided to open the door, and we immediately began this tug of war over it. I soon realized that this fight was going to happen, and I had my adrenaline pumping. The door was released, and the fight started. I was blocking his hands when he grabbed my shirt and pulled it over my head. I couldn't see what was happening, but I knew instantly where he was and swung a right hook that hit him square in the nose. He started to bleed and fell to the ground.

I was able to see again, and I had the upper hand. As his blood started to make a mess all over the entrance to the apartment complex, I felt in control. I had to throw a few more punches to keep him on the ground; he wouldn't stay down. At some point, the police were called, and I took the elevator up to her place to tell her what had happened, so she went down. The police arrived, and he said it was just a Super Bowl fight between friends, and the police let it go. I had no injuries, and I was back on speaking terms with the girl I loved, although she had moved on and had no intention of being back with me. I should have just been a man and made love to her that night. Sometimes I can be too polite and Christian. The thing I want most in life is my other half, and I fought for her. I won. I defended her right to make money for herself anyway she chooses, and I got nothing for it, but this story. Later on, he would call the police on her after a night she had following a rave where she messed around with her sister's ex-boyfriend, and she would have the scare of her life. I moved on and tried to find my own way in LA.

I had no access to the real nightlife, and I had no ability to persuade anyone. I was just another guy who thought he was good-looking and was willing to give up my life for a chance at fame. Living in a bigger apartment all by myself was lonely; I had more space to be alone in. I remember getting a job working at the Beverly Center, working in retail; it is a painful memory. I had no education and made no money; I was suffering from my DUI. I took the bus for .25 cents to work a basic job; on the other hand, my ex-girlfriend was making 5-10k in Vegas, being a stripper, etc. Life isn't fair. The sales of sex are incredible. Another term for sex is love, and women get to sell love—often earning more per hour than a doctor who sometimes saves lives.

When I was younger, my family was fighting, and it was easy to smoke weed, get high, and escape reality. As time went on, that same way of escaping reality was having fun, and by fun, I would go out to clubs and bars and drink, and meet people. That is something I was really good at, and for the most part, it never got old to me.

One of those times, while I was living in this location, things got pretty serious. I was having a great time at the afterparty; everyone was drinking more, doing cocaine, and talking about whatever we do at afterparties. Next thing I know, the sun is coming up, and it rose quickly and got really hot—it was about 11 am. Time to leave the party, and I was careless. Good thing I wasn't driving after walking past the Beverly Center, which was about 4-5 blocks from the party. I was so dehydrated that I thought it would be a good idea to just lie down near the bus stop for a little bit. The next thing I remember is waking up in the back of an ambulance, and they used ammonia to wake me up. Once I gained consciousness, I asked, "Where am I?"

They told me an ambulance was coming! I panicked and said, "Get me out of here. I cannot afford this!" To my amazement, they let me go; they told me to get food and water. I went to McDonald's, came home, and slept. It was a traumatic memory that really shows me how long I've been living like an alcoholic and drug addict. So, of course, I secretly knew this already, and I jumped at the opportunity because my mother was right: I hated my job and wished I could finish some sort of school. She offered to pay for my room and board while I take a year off and go to school at Paul Mitchell to learn how to be a hair stylist. Now, moving back home to live with my mom at this point was very hard to accept. The other side was that she was engaged to a man who had a 5-bedroom house and was a very cool guy. We were like the Brady Bunch. He had three daughters; my mom had three sons. I still couldn't drive, so I had to be driven to school every day. One of his daughters also wanted to be a hair stylist, so she enrolled around the same time as I.

Back to the Bay Area

I felt awkward about the whole situation, but when was my life not awkward after living in San Francisco? I learned that being awkward can just mean you are out of place, but being out of place doesn't always mean you are not in a situation that will benefit your life. Living with my mom in a big house was always a dream of mine as a kid. Her man is a really good person, and to this day, I admire his honesty, tenacity, and commitment to being a good person. He lived on both sides of the spectrum. I just happened to catch him on the good side, which was great because he understood both worlds. He was in love with my mom, and I thought he was the best person for her. I lived there for about two months before I found a roommate in Walnut Creek.

It was also awkward at first, living with a young guy like me who went to the gym, had a regular job, drove a truck, drank beer, and cooked at home. I lived in a tiny room and paid half the rent. It was like two guys who didn't grow up together or share the same vibe—there was this unspoken tension, maybe even a subconscious competition. I don't know. But having to share the same space felt weird at first; even something as simple as watching TV together was awkward. We never fought till the end. I started to smoke pot in my room because I didn't want to leave my room; it was like I was hiding out there. I definitely wish I were somewhere else. This wasn't my happy place. I would get picked up by my mother and go to school in a new Mercedes or sometimes an Aston Martin. I was attending school at Paul Mitchell with girls who had just graduated from high school, along with some who were mothers or even grandmothers, showcasing a diverse range of people.

The first part of school was really awesome; it was the prep, and everything was fun and exciting. We got lockers and a whole kit with everything we would need to get started doing hair. I still have my box, which is now decorated with all sorts of cool stickers that make it look like it was tattooed. I went to school five days a week, and it was 40 hours each week. I started school at the exact time that the movie "Don't Mess with the Zohan" came out, and we all went as a school to watch that film.

I would make some really cool friends whom I still keep in touch with today. One of them, whom I nicknamed Blondie, was a great friend to me. We went to see Britney Spears in concert, had way too much fun, and I ended up in the drunk tank before being released. I was wearing white pants, and they became blue because of all the blue jeans that were grinding on me. We were fortunate to reunite but ended up on the wrong train home, nearly getting stuck in Brisbane, and we took the last B.A.R.T. train back to Walnut Creek. She made school much better, and she was amazing to me. One time, we hit an off-ramp on the freeway going about 80 miles per hour. The tires screeched, and for a moment, I was genuinely afraid for my life, but somehow, we made it through safely.

She earned the name Blondie because she was so blonde, and in life, she was blonde as well. I want to share the story that touched my heart forever; it's the logic of her mind that endears her to me. This beautiful angel with heart-shaped ass and baby blue eyes from the upper mid-west fell in love with a Mexican who did not have a green card and was deported. With her broken heart, she decided not to marry him, because she wasn't ready for that sort of commitment. So, she packed her bags at 19 and moved to Mexico to be with him. The house she was living in wasn't very big, and she shared it with nine other family members. After nine months of living there, she said she just learned how to speak Spanish; she said she could open her mouth and Spanish would come out, but she didn't know how.

I used to think it would have been easier if she had just married him. She is such a kind and trusting soul, like a baby deer—so gentle and soft. I don't think she really knew what life in Mexico was going to be like. But I have a lot of respect for her for staying with the man she loved and enduring it all. I'm sure it was worth it to her. So that is part of the reason I call her Blondie. I actually had to reach out and call her before I started to write this part of my book. I wanted to tell her I was going to write about her. It was pleasant to hear her voice. I love her. She's such a sweet girl.

We both had crushes on each other at the time, and we both had reasons for us to just stay friends. However, she still loved her man in Mexico, and I felt like I was pure corruption. I have this idea about myself that just isn't true—that I'll only end up hurting good girls, so I should stay away from them because I'm bad news. I've always felt like a bad boy with a heart of gold. Still, deep down, I know I'll make a good father. More than anything, I want to own a home, raise a family, and live a happily-ever-after kind of life. For the most part, while I was in school, I really just focused on getting a high passing score on all my tests. This was very important to me. It was finally school that my parents were paying for, and I wanted to make my mother proud. Towards the end of school, I loosened up a bit and started to hang out with my classmates outside of school.

Actually, it was one of my teachers. She used to live in Vegas; she was an "Entertainer," and now she was teaching class. She was older and knew how to talk to me; she would give me extra help when I needed it. I was special and needed that attention. I was one of six guys in a school of 230 girls: three straight and three gay. I was supposed to move to Los Angeles and become a celebrity, cutting and styling the hair of other stars. Yes, I have the courage to be a star, and yes, I have a star tattooed on my balls. Now I wish I had been more of a badass in class. Although I was pretty badass, sometimes I felt like rising against the establishment, but I kept a low profile. So, what happened was she cracked the code and made me more approachable to all the other girls. I didn't want to fuck this up. Although I really wanted to jump into the love that was waiting for me. There was this really pretty, slim Middle Eastern girl there with an older guy, and I felt she deserved better; she and I had that chemical magnetic passion. We both knew it was wrong, but we did it anyway. Thinking back to that moment, I felt loved. I felt it was right. I tried to keep it a secret, but I think they knew. So, when I was living in San Francisco before I moved to LA, I booked this MAC cosmetic job where we were shirtless models with painted faces for a big party they were filming. They had all these incredible models who were fully covered in MAC makeup, and one day, MAC came to our school and did a presentation.

While the whole school was watching, I appeared in this video they were showcasing as the big deal of the year, and I felt vindication. Some of the girls cheered for me, and that felt amazing. I felt justified in my ego—I knew who I was, and I stood by it. That also reminds me of the day that the whole school gathered together, and they had us write down our goals, including what we wanted to do with our hair styling career. Most people mentioned basic goals like making 50k or being self-supporting; some expressed a desire to open their own salon one day. Those were the brave ones who said that. When it came to me, my list was much longer than everyone else's. I must have seemed greedy, proud, or boastful, which isn't fair to me, but people were amazed. My list went something like this: I want to style hair for New York Fashion Week, the Victoria's Secret Fashion Show, multiple covers for Vogue, Cosmo, GQ, Playboy, W, Vman, and all the major magazines in fashion. I aspire to style photo shoots for Gucci, Prada, Versace, LV, Dior, and all the major labels. I envision participating in fashion weeks worldwide, including Brazil, Paris, London, Germany, and Japan. I aim to style hair for red-carpet parties in LA, such as the Oscars, Golden Globes, SAG Awards, and all the major movie premieres. I want to style hair for films shot globally, allowing me to travel and establish my name.

Eventually, I would love to open my own salons in Paris, New York, London, Germany, Miami, Vegas, Los Angeles, etc. I want to own a house in Malibu and a penthouse in New York. I have big goals I plan to accomplish. Why do I want to accomplish all of this, you may ask? It's exciting, it's creative, and it's what will allow me to showcase my unique strengths fully. Looking back at it, I have accomplished a percentage of this list as of today, and I am still working on it, thankfully.

One of my friends just texted me saying she booked an audition because I styled her hair yesterday. So, my classmates had this impression of me, and when they saw me on the big screen, they sort of had to swallow their doubts. This world can judge you or say what they think the truth is about you, but in the end, it matters how you feel about yourself. People couldn't change my opinion of myself back then; I am the only one who talks shit about myself that actually hurts me. I try to be nice to myself and remember that I followed my heart and I gave in to my wildest dreams, I fell into the abyss, I chased Alice into Wonderland, and I never looked back. I was wearing this 2-carat diamond ring I got for my 26th birthday, which was a yellow and brown fancy diamond. I set it in platinum and put 3 white diamonds on either side to make it look like a human eye. When the light hit the diamond just right, it looked green to me, and I've always loved the comic book character Green Lantern. So, to me, this was my Mr Cool ring. It made me feel like I had superpowers.

I noticed one day that some women flash a diamond ring at you to show you their status in life, and now I had a ring that I would wave back with a smile. Now the teacher, who was an entertainer in Vegas, called me one night while she was buzzed on Champagne. She was with the most beautiful girl in school, and they both invited me over to Dublin, where she was living. I was instantly put into a fantasy. I never thought this day would come, nor did I want this day to come, but it came, and I went. The three of us were all back at her apartment. We were drinking and talking, and laughing. I had my bags packed for San Diego or LA, and I was to leave the next morning. We were all in bed, fooling around, playing with each other's bodies. They were comparing, teasing, and the prettiest girl in school completely outshone the older Vegas teacher. I made the fatal mistake of not giving them equal attention, and just like that, the fantasy ended. It was time to go to sleep.

But I couldn't. The three of us had even compared diamond sizes before bed, like it was all part of the strange, dreamy night. I kept getting up to drink more, thinking it would help me pass out. And then I did the most embarrassing thing ever—not just missing the chance to sleep with both girls. I actually pissed the bed.

I drank too much to fall asleep, and when I woke up, the bed was wet and my ring was gone. Now the girls made me promise never to tell anyone I was over there before I came, and now with my ring gone and me in So Cal, I was sort of fucked here. I didn't want to get the girls in trouble, but I knew one of them stole my ring. When I got back, she didn't find it. She even suggested that I didn't have the ring in the first place. She asked if I had insurance on the ring. I looked at her, crazy, like, can you really have insurance on rings? Now I know. Now the Vegas chick is the one that I think took it because I pissed her bed accidentally. She was 100x more attractive; she had perfect boobs and double Ds with beautiful nipples too. Straight girls would have gone down on this girl for hours because I know I would have for days. So, two weeks ago, goodbye and no ring; my mom had Jedi senses, and I wanted to tell her so badly what had happened. Now, I loved this ring so much; it was my pride and joy. I had plans to give the diamond to my future wife because, honestly, I wasn't sure if I would ever be able to afford a 2-carat diamond ring on my own.

I would have been more than happy to give it to the woman I love, and I hope she would be proud to wear it. I still have the GIA report and would love to replace it one day. The platinum weighed 26 grams; it was heavy.

Now, this story may gross you out, so you can skip ahead if you want. This ring meant so much to me that when I got my DUI in SF, they took me to jail, and while I was drunk, I swallowed my ring because I thought the police would steal my ring. Yes, I did have to fish it out, and I found it, it was easy. I had refused to eat any of the food in jail. I was used to 5-star restaurants, and I thought it was rude that they wanted me to eat this SF County Jail food. It was horrible. I got out after 3 days, with all that in mind, I told my mother that these two women had done to me, because I was the victim here. My mom went straight up to the hot one who also worked at the school and confronted her in the most gangster way. My mom doesn't play; she's from Mexico. It was very sad that it all happened that way. I would have loved for the three of us to have had an easy time, and we all would have kept it a secret, and I would still have my ring. This is why I waited so long to open up at school.

I had about two months left to finish. Luckily, Blondie was still my friend, but my almost stepsister was probably mortified. We never really spoke except for hi and bye. I keep my distance from people when I know that one day there will probably be no reason for us to talk to each other. I feel bad about that; it's just that I don't want to seem fake, and if I think we won't be friends later, I won't fake or force a dialogue. With Blondie, everything came natural; we became friends for life. Now the whole school was going to know what had happened. I was mildly afraid of what people would say about me behind my back, and if they would talk about me peeing the bed. No matter what they said about me, it wouldn't hurt because this was nothing compared to what they didn't know about me. I am still a man with a dream, and I will continue to pursue my dream until I achieve it. So, as the time came to take the state board test, I was ready to move out of the apartment I was living in with the Craigslist roommate. He was normal; I was the crazy artist that not everyone could understand. He made me feel uncomfortable because he was so normal.

News got out of school, now that the drama was at an all-time high, and I wanted to prove to everyone that I was going to be a success. The only way to do that would be to pass my state board on the first shot. We had to wake up at 5 am to be at the testing grounds by 6 am, take the practical portion, and then take the written. All the girls were freaking out and crying about the test; it seemed strange to me. I was like, why am I not freaking out? They were so convincing that there should have been something to fear, but it turned out there was nothing to worry about. I got my results the same day I took the test; I was now immediately licensed to do hair. I was so excited; I called my mom, and she was thrilled. We were both in heaven. My cousin Rachel was able to be my hair model, which I am grateful for. I took my license back to school and waved it around like it was the American Flag. I was so proud, and I again felt vindication. I took my life seriously, and I passed my test. Some of the top people failed the test and had to retake it. Not to mention, my possible stepsister didn't pass the first time. Having a silver spoon doesn't mean you take things seriously.

I should also mention that this was back when Ed Hardy was still famous and cool. My club friends in Walnut Creek were promoting an Ed Hardy fashion show, and I got the chance to walk in my first runway show while I was still in school. I even styled the hair of this gorgeous model, who ended up becoming a friend. I gave her a rad mohawk that night, and we danced together well into the midnight hours.

San Francisco Round 2

Right out of beauty school, I was hired to work at Di Pietro Todd Salon in San Francisco, allowing me to move back to the city. I remember finding an apartment for $1,100 on Mason and Bush. This has been my favorite spot to live in the city so far. It was my own apartment, complete with a walk-in closet that connected to a charming little bathroom, which featured a shower where I hung my disco ball. All my clothes fit perfectly into the closet, and my close friend gave me his king-size bed, which would make a great centerpiece for this studio apartment. The building itself was very classy, and I felt very privileged to live in this apartment. I wanted to live a good life, work, and make money. I believe I was making minimum wage plus tips at the salon. As a second job, I worked for California Dream Dancers, and on my very first day in the apartment, I had two dance gigs lined up. I thought it was one hell of a way to come back to San Francisco.

My apartment contained little more than a bag full of clothes for the weekend. There was no bed yet, just a blanket. That night of dancing led me to a bachelorette party that went wild. After I danced for the girls, there were three of them that I really liked and who liked me. Since I knew the city so well, we went to a party where we were greeted fairly. Whenever I arrive with a group of girls, like ten of them, it's going to be a red-carpet entrance with free drinks. Not that we needed more drinks; I was already buzzed and excited about moving back to the city.

I was a free bird again, and that night I really took advantage of my freedom. I was being playful with the three girls whose attention I had, and later that night, we claimed a table to ourselves where we created our own dirty dancing movie. We got to the point of no return, and I was so brave to pull out my cock and receive a blow job right there in the middle of Harry Denton's club. When we were discovered, we had to leave, and the night could have ended there. I wanted to take that special girl back to my new apartment, so she agreed and we found our way. The next thing that was to happen completely took me by surprise. The last time this occurred, I was just a child. Can anyone guess what I'm talking about?

As we were fucking, I started sucking her breast and, I tasted breast milk for the first time as an adult. I was completely surprised. She didn't seem to act like a young mother; it had a sweetness similar to honey milk, which was definitely better than cow's milk. That is a night I will never forget. I came back to San Francisco with a vengeance, and I thought I was ready for this new job and title I had as a hair-stylist. With wild oats sown and a newfound freedom back in a city I was comfortable in, I started to rebuild my life again. When I was hired at the salon, I was told that I would have to change my name. I started to laugh as I thought it was a joke. They were serious; they had two other people with the same name, and they maintained a policy of non-confusion. So, when you mention a stylist's name, you know exactly who you're talking about. Now, as I started off as an assistant, I needed to change my name. I called my mom and was like, 'What is this?' She told me I should just go for it—that people who complete the program become master stylists and can earn over $200,000 a year.

So, I loved Egyptian History and wanted to be a pharaoh. I also loved money, and the Latin term for money was "dinero." I mixed the two words together and made "Deairo."

I had the choice of color or cutting in the Di Pietro Todd Salon program. I knew that color stylists made more money, and I was all about the money. Again, I was surrounded by women and gay men. This salon was very strict, but they have an incredible program; they are a L'Oréal certified training facility worldwide. I was really lucky to be chosen to work for them, and again, I didn't know that I was working at one of the best salons. I did, but I didn't; my heart was in LA, and I was just a broken human surviving on my own. One of the other color students was a beautiful red-headed girl who was just 19 and recently married. Although she was unable to take time off work for a honeymoon, she acted as if that was normal. When she told me that the salon would not give her the time off, I was in complete shock and did not realize how someone could accept this type of treatment. For me, I was still unsure that being a hairstylist would be the answer to my future financial problems.

I still didn't really want to be a hair stylist, and I was now in boot camp for training to be a Navy Seal of hair. I was working at the Fillmore location, and we serviced clients from Pacific Heights. I worked upstairs in the color department, and my job was washing color bowls, folding foils, cleaning, shampooing, and bringing clients coffee, tea, and hot water. I was an errand boy at 28. Working with older or rich, powerful women, being responsible for giving them pleasure at the same time, while using a shampoo bowl that can be uncomfortable, I struggled. Sometimes, I left color on the other side of their heads that I could not see. This was a big deal because I would then have to shampoo them all over again. Rich people prefer things to be done the right way the first time. I was not comfortable, and I hated my mom for putting me in this position. I felt like this was crazy. Why couldn't I just be a stripper and dance for people and make $500 a day and drink and have sex with the girls who wanted to fuck me? I was used to being spoiled. I was the prize in the world, and I was no good at being a humble servant. Making minimum wage plus tips and having to sell these people expensive products, I just couldn't understand how they could spend $300 on hair color and another $100 on shampoo.

Having short conversations with these people was tough because we were on completely different ends of the spectrum. These women want to discuss dogs and children, the play they saw last week, and the weather. Some women get a gay vibe and ask me gay stuff, and then I get offended. It's been a real confusing situation. I would get the 'Are you gay?' question so many times in life, it used to drive me crazy. Then I would say, 'If I've confused you, then I've won.' Sometimes I would be asked if I was gay out in a bar, and at that point, I would just kiss the girl or reach around and grab her pussy, and then that would be my answer. She would feel that I was going for pussy and not cock and balls. I used to show up to work sober and ready for anything. As time went on, I would do as I've always done: I would party and show up to work still drunk or a little hung over. I did my best to balance.

Every Monday, the salon required us to have four models to practice color on. When we first started, they taught us how to blow-dry hair; I was only comfortable holding the brush and blow-dryer the way that felt comfortable to me. They would have me extend my arm way farther than normal and hold the blow dryer in a way that was so uncomfortable, it was Nazi hair boot camp. Now, having four models every Monday was a real challenge. We had to find new paying clients who had natural red hair with 70% gray, and they had to pay. Not to mention, this was a working day, and everyone was at work, so we needed them to call in, take time off, and pay for us to do their hair. Everyone who was an assistant there was a very strong-willed person with a strong sense of style and confidence. It was the most eclectic group of young stylists, and they would read to one another and compete against each other, just as we did in hair school. I wish this were a sport like soccer or baseball, where all I had to do was run faster or be more physical. I always resort to my strength because this is what I have. In today's world, my strength means nothing unless I'm beating up my ex-girlfriend's boyfriend, and even then, it's not enough.

Maybe it was good when I was lifting girls over my head during the bachelorette parties. If I were lucky enough to be on the cover of Men's Health magazine, then my body would matter. Some girls love men with a great body, although I think they all prefer a good heart, then mounds of cash, then a pretty face, then a nice body. I guess what I'm saying is I'm out of my element here doing assistant work for the richest people in San Francisco. I was meant to be paid to party and be a socialite, or a public speaker who helps young people realize that the life I was living following my heart was not the best choice. There is no guarantee that I will find true love, buy a house, or have children. I was able to survive for about seven months working at this salon. I'm not sure if I quit or if I was fired; I'm fairly certain I was let go. It's like it wasn't my dream job, and I was in the most elite school in California, and I was still just a kid in college with dreams of being a star. After working at Di Pietro Todd salon, I was able to work for a salon my friend had just opened, called Aqua Di Roma. This salon was part of a health and wellness center, offering massage therapy, facials, nutritional advice, and colonics. I was the first hairstylist to work there, and I was extremely excited. I felt like I was the manager, and I thought I could transition from this A-list salon into being my own stylist. One of the issues with the salon was that it was commission-based, and to this day, it remains my job to find new clients, which is always an ordeal. I wanted to specialize in blondes and keeping blondes blonde. For natural blondes, level 6 and up, it was easy to do the work.

I found a girl who was from Israel, and she had blonde ends and black roots. I found her in the mall and told her I would be happy to do her hair. She had a birthday coming up, and she wanted to be a perfect blonde for her special day. So, she comes in for her appointment with half off offered, and I start to work. I got 7 levels of lift, and she was still brassy. This was taking a long time; she had a lot of hair. She started to realize I was not an expert in bleaching and toning. I normally use high-lift bleach and tone from L'Oreal, and it works perfectly for natural blondes. This case turned into a nightmare for me at work; my boss had to call in another hair stylist from another salon, and he showed me what I was doing wrong. I was taking too big of sections, not saturating the hair evenly.

The client was crying, and it showed that I was not ready to work for myself. I promised myself that I would never take unnatural blondes to blonde. This would save me the nightmare that just happened from ever happening again. I lost my confidence, and I lost respect in this new salon. They ended up hiring another guy quickly to be able to oversee my work, and they assured me that it was for the best. We had a fundraiser that was in the Trans America building, and that was the first and only time I got to visit the top of the pyramid in San Francisco.

Bachelorette & Birthday Parties

So, I created this routine because most of the Bachlorette & Birthday parties were in hotel rooms. I would come in dressed in a suit and tie, knocking on the door as if I were hotel security. Actually, first, I would have the girl who hired me come meet me privately and pay me. I would then let her know I would be back up there shortly to start the routine. I would say, "And make sure the girls are drinking and feeling frisky so we have lots of fun." Most, if not all, the girls liked it when I danced for their friends; it was like punishing the girls with pleasure. So, I told her to place the money on the girls she wanted me to dance for. I would get paid better, and it was more fun that way for everyone, so no one looked thirsty for a cock tease.

My parties started with - The door opens.

"Hi ladies, we're getting complaints from the neighbors. We need to keep it down a little bit. Is it someone's birthday?" All the girls would say yes!! Oh, that's cool.

Then my music starts, which is "Bad to the Bone," a classic dancer song, and all the girls start to scream. I get a chair and have the special lady sit down so all the attention is on her. Then Genuine would play next - "Come and ride my pony."

I start to take off my clothes, while dancing to the beat, until my shirt is off. I look exactly like the guy on the cover of this book. I pull the blindfold out of my underwear and blind fold the BDAY girl for Bride to be. She can no longer see. I have a few tricks up my sleeve, one of them being a King-size

Snickers bar, which they no longer make. I would let all the other girls know I was putting this in my underwear; just by doing it, they would all see and start to laugh. I lived off the laughter. The more they screamed, the better the party. It's pretty tough for me to get aroused without intimacy, and this show has no intimacy until later. So while she is blind folded and the other girls are screaming and seeing what's happening, I am now without shoes because it's not sexy taking off shoes, so she doesn't see that part. Now I am standing in front of her with just my underwear on and a Snickers bar in my undies. I take the bride's hands and place them on my body where she can feel my chest, and I pull her hands down slowly to feel my smooth body and my chiseled abs. The next thing her mind tells her is that she's going to feel my Rock-Hard Man parts.

By this time, all the girls are going crazy and laughing because they can see that the bride is getting tricked. She doesn't really want to touch me; she is in love with another man. So, 90% of them pull away as I force them to touch my candy bar. The bride is bright red and laughing, and I let her and her friends gain their composure. I take the Snickers bar out of my underwear and open it up. I grab the bride by the back of her hair and get a handful.

I say out loud, "Now open your mouth."

This sets off everyone; they are dying with laughter and screaming. It's the most fun I've ever had with random strangers in the celebration of marriage. The farthest I go is to make the candy bar touch her lips, and by that point, she takes off her blind fold out of sheer curiosity. How could her friends let me do this to her? She sees the candy bar and laughs and realizes it's all fun and games; nothing happened. While she is calming down, I ask her who she wants me to dance with. She points at her best friend, or the one who hired me, the biggest instigator, and then the fun begins. This would be my show for up to 200-300 shows over my lifetime. The girls were so ready to party; they offered me shots, and the music played for 45 minutes to an hour. I was able to pick the girls up and have them ride on me while standing up, legs around my hips and arms around my neck. It's a great position to be in for both of us. I then take it up a notch. I am able to get my arms underneath he legs and lift her all the way up so her kitty cat is right in my face. I make sure to kiss the kitty. A lot of the girls will be screaming because I am strong enough to lift them up, whereas most of them are not expecting this to happen. It's like all the girls can feel what is happening to the one I am dancing with. I bring handcuffs to the party, which is always fun. She is left fairly helpless; it's so controlling. I also have whip cream to place on their neck, and that gives me a reason to lick the whip cream off of her body. A lot of bumping and grinding, and the room gets hot. One of my best memories is when a stripper girl was getting married, and she brought all her stripper girl friends to the hotel room. These girls tipped a lot of money, and it was extra turnt up that night. I've danced with ladies from all nationalities and had a lot of fun! One time, the bride-to-be was allergic to peanuts, and so while she was blind folded and her friends saw the Snickers bar, they screamed, "Stop! You will kill her!" I was like, "What?" Lucky, no allergic reaction started or took place. The was a very serious moment, and glad nothing bad happened. Obviously, I was only there to have fun and make it memorable.

Right now, I just looked online and found a company that was using my picture from when I used to dance. They said they would rehire me, so I'm considering dancing again. While I am between jobs again, I do love the work; it's fun when you are in control, and women get to treat you like a piece of meat. It feels like the most natural place to be in. It's very special and loving in a way. The amount of acceptance vs what normal rejection feels like in the real world. One of my favorite feelings in the world. I wish it would never end :) kisses! Sometimes I was a Cowboy with a black Stetson hat or a police officer. Fireman was very popular too.

IDAHO or Not the HO

After realizing that I still needed more training to master color, I was hit with some surprising news from my mother. She was in contact with the man she had cheated on my father with, which led to our family's divorce, and they still maintained a friendship. She would start to plan living in Idaho because it was an easier life than the expensive California. My middle brother is fully supported by my mother and the government due to his disability. He was living in Danville and was not taking his medication. he had called the police and proceeded to let them know that he was stronger and bigger than them. He was later arrested that night, and my mother had to come to rescue him; he was just bored that day. My mother managed to rescue all of us boys. While I was living in Walnut Creek, finishing school, attending beauty school, and working, I was stripping, which my mother and potential stepdad were aware of.

They once took me to a job in Ruby Hills and picked me up after. I had a job in San Francisco with these Asian girls, which was really fun. After dancing all night, I really wanted to get laid, and somehow I thought the more I drank, the more likely I thought I was to get laid. Which is really not true. What ended up happening was that my only Stetson cowboy hat was kept as a souvenir, and I was blacked out drunk with a dying battery. I called my mom and told her I was on the streets near Bart in SF, and I couldn't walk. She had to come look for me and drove all the streets till she found me. So, I am just as bad as my brother, if not worse, in a different way, whom I will love forever. (family thing) Now my mom's current partner gave her an ultimatum: Your boys (young men) are driving me crazy; you have to choose me or them. So, my mom chose us.

While I was working in San Francisco, an older man came in and wanted a haircut. He had only a few hairs on his head and more on the sides. He paid the $60 for the haircut and gave me a $20 tip. Little did I know that he was going to marry my mother shortly, and he was the man with whom we lived in Hawaii as kids. I felt tricked, and I was oddly shocked. I still had my heart in LA. My mother had found a way for me to work and live in LA. She found a salon called Frederic Fekkai, and they were looking for an assistant. This again is another salon that takes three years or more to become a stylist and has a rigorous training program that would have probably suffocated me. However, it was a way for me to avoid moving to Idaho. I am a city person, and I need the city to live in. I make friends fast and short-lived. We are friends as long as we are together, but when we leave, neither you nor I will contact each other. I may contact you, but it's a city thing.

While I was in LA, I went to the interview, and they called me back for a second interview. I was staying with an ex-girlfriend who was a stripper in SF and came to LA. She had a place downtown. She was platinum blonde, and we have always been friends. I met her living in San Francisco. She gave me the best threesome of my life, at least so far. We had sex for 2-3 days straight and didn't leave the house. The second girl was so amazing. I was elated. To this day, just thinking about that sex and how it came to be excites me. So, I was staying with her and I got the call to come back for a second interview. The salon wanted to see how I blow-dry curly hair straight. I needed a hair model, and from the last time I lived in LA, I knew that people in LA would be willing to help me with this task if they knew it would help me get a job.

We went to the meetings on Robertson, and I found a person with curly hair looking through the window. We had to wait to ask until the meeting was over. So, we decided to go to the Abby and look there as well. We looked around and didn't find anything. She was getting tired and asked to use the bathroom. So, I waited for her and kept waiting and waiting. I yelled in there like, "What's going on?"

She was like, "These women are all in the bathroom stall taking forever."

I was like, "Do they have curly hair, lol?"

When they came out, one of them did, and so she said, "Can you help my friend out? He needs someone with curly hair to get a job at this salon."

She came outside and we spoke. She was an older lady, about 43, and she was well off. She said she had a skin care salon in Beverly Hills. So, I kept her card and we spoke the next day. I asked her to come in, and she did. I was able to make the second interview, and more importantly, I made a new friend. I was better at talking with her and asking her questions about her life. Her hair was frizzy and a challenge for me to work with, although it looked good in the end.

The salon thanked me and let me leave. She was right behind me and realized that I was about to walk home or to a bus stop. She asked me if I needed a ride, and I realized then and there that we had a future together as she let me into her

SL 550. I had felt this feeling before in life, and it was returning to me again. I should have known when she set her LV purse on Frederic Fekki's countertop that this was going to change my life. I wasn't sure if it was the new job at an equally crazy salon or if it was her. She drove me up to Sunset Blvd., and I told her I was going to have to walk that trip, and she was very empathic towards me. I was to take the second bus all the way downtown, and she let me know that if I were to need a place to stay again in LA, I could possibly stay with her. The trip to LA was a success. I would have to wait and hear back from the salon to see if I passed. My mom was now moving on, her relationship was ending, and she had a backup plan and escape route, as she always does. I was still in my spot in SF, and I was the witness to my mother's wedding; only a small number of people knew this wedding was taking place. The wedding took place at City Hall in San Francisco, and we held the celebration at the Mark Hopkins Hotel. After that, they had a room for cake and champagne.

I sort of learned to just go with the flow and let people be who they are. It's too much work to try and change anybody unless they want to change. I thought that maybe he was going to be the one that my mother really wanted and was going to live with forever. My mother was paying my rent as my life in the salon in San Francisco was quickly evaporating. I was able to learn how to do extensions while I was in San Francisco and was certified in Shrink Links, which are a very popular type of hair extension. My mother took away my rent money and said we're all moving to Idaho, all the brothers, and we're going to be a family up there. I was freaking out; I could not live in a small town with nothing going on. I said I would go ahead and visit with her, and we did. It was beautiful, and it was devoid of city life, with clean air and beautiful snow that sparkled. This is a place where celebrities retreat when they want to escape from LA or NYC. This was no place for me to live. I returned to the Bay Area and had some time to figure out my next move.

I was turning 30 this year, and I was no longer in my 20s, which made me feel like life was passing me by and I was a failure; I had nothing to show for my life. I did get my driver's license back, and I was able to drive. I had hardly any money to my name, and I was either going to have to live in Idaho or take care of myself. I had no clients, and dancing wasn't enough money to live off. My mother had me by the balls, or at least she thought she did; she wanted me to live in Idaho. I had time to talk with the lady in Beverly Hills and made plans to come to LA and stay with my best friend, whom I had met modeling in San Francisco. We had both met on a job that painted us head to toe in gold for the Oscars, and we were like statues for this high-end party.

We met when I was living in Walnut Creek at my second apartment right before I moved to the city. This would become a lifelong friendship, and I consider him family, like a brother to me. So, while I was in LA, I got to see what ladies in Beverly Hills really expected from me. I was truly starting to freak out about where I would live and where I would work. This is a theme in my life, and it's really a tough feeling. I have been lucky in the past, and I find a way to survive even though I have to sell my soul or break all my Christian boundaries, which makes me party and drink, and have fun to forget about reality. I'm at my friend's house, and I call her; she lives way up in the hills of Benedict Canyon. She offers to pay for my taxi ride up there, so I do. The taxi comes, and we make a right off Sunset Blvd. We take a winding road and keep going, and going, and going. I was freaking out, it was dark, and I had no idea how deep in the hills I was. I came upon a house that was completely surrounded by flowers and trees; it was like a rainforest surrounding the house. I rang the doorbell a few times, and there was no response.

I took a look around and made sure the address was correct. She comes to open the door and invites me in. As soon as you walk in, you see a collection of picture frames, and everyone who is important in her life is there. I notice her picture with George W. Bush first, and that sets a tone in my mind: Wow, this lady has some real connections to the world. Something I had no idea how to achieve in life. I was intrigued by her power and her success. I was finally in LA, where I had always dreamed of living. I was with a potentially wonderful lady who seemed to want to be part of my life, and this was my chance to learn and grow, and have a new Guardian Angel. First, I took a tour of the 5-bedroom, 3-bath house; she showed me her office and the spare room in the front wing of the house. Next was the living room and the kitchen in a big open space, sort of connected. Down the hall is her daughter's room, which was news to me; she had a workout room and then the master bedroom at the back. She explained to me that I could only come over then because her daughter was out visiting friends, and when the daughter was away, the mother would play.

She offered me something to drink, and since both of our favorites were champagne, that's how we started. I was immediately feeling like I was lured into a cougar's den, and I know it's a dangerous place to be; I was willing to slay the dragon to find a new start in LA. As we continued to drink, we were having a good time talking, and she gave off the vibe of a hardcore New Yorker. She has a way with words. We take a break, and she needs to leave the room for a phone call, so I take the chance to call my friend, but there's no answer. I called back, but there was no reception. I call another friend, and he answers—my close, red-headed Jewish friend. I'm a bit nervous, slightly panicked, because I don't know what kind of drama I'm about to get myself into.

So, I ask him, "Bro, this cougar wants to hit; she's offering me a place to hang until I get on my feet."

He says, "Is she hot?"

I'm like, "She's kinda. Like she has a big rack, and she probably was when she was younger."

He went like, "Well fuck it, bro. What you got to lose?"

"The worst that can happen to you is you got some older pussy?"

"Fuck you're right. I don't know if it will work."

I don't want this to get all weird, so I'm like, "Yes or no?"

He's like, "Yes."

I hear her walking down the hallway.

"Okay, I've got to go. Thanks, bro!!"

Beverly Hills

Yes, I'm sure. I already made my choice; I've always wanted to move to LA. I know, I don't have any money, and I'm not going to have to pay rent. You know, I came to LA for my 21st birthday when everyone else goes to Vegas. LA is a place where dreams can come true. What am I going to do in Idaho? You know I'll go crazy up there; this is Beverly Hills. If I'm going to be a hairstylist, I might as well be in LA, where I can meet celebrities. Who knows, maybe I can become an actor and do TV commercials or even a movie one day! Yes, I am doing this; this is the life I chose, and there's no turning back. You know I love you. Stop trying to control my life. This was especially hard for my mother to accept; it's not her place to choose what I do with my life. However, this whole living situation reminded me of the incident that occurred when I was 17, living in Marin City, working for that day spa where the aesthetician took advantage of me. The age gap here is 13 years in Beverly Hills and a whole world of knowledge. This was an escape; it was playing in the devil's playground. It was a cycle that reappeared in my life. I wonder if this type of cycle will appear in your life? You have to be keen enough to spot the danger zones. Older woman who does facials same exact circumstances.

We were both alcoholics, and she was just a very talented one who could keep up with the Joneses, and I was a young Latin/white kid with a pretty face and abs and a star tattoo on his balls. I was emotionally scared and willing to die. How much worse could this be? I figured anyone who knows me and knows that I have a star tattoo on my balls should put me in a different category. You can't think I'm normal; I have nothing to show for my life, just my paintings and my body. I am still alive.

This aesthetician had my mom beat; she made it to Beverly Hills, owned a home, was on TV, and made millions of dollars. I choose to follow my dreams, and it bothers her when I do. I cannot do what other people want me to do; I have to do what I want. I will do a trade and share parts of myself that people do not deserve, and that's the old me. It's just that part of life is so hard to give up; it keeps coming back. The normal world doesn't pay enough money for anyone to survive without a good college education, truly. My education is worldly, and I'm so tired of being poor or broke. I am frustrated at the God that my parents loved for making my family suffer; that God did nothing for me. It was a trap not to live life to the fullest and not experience the most amazing things in life. I packed up a U-Haul truck all by myself, with all my belongings, and drove down to Beverly Hills.

I was strong enough to move everything by myself, and nothing was going to stop me from pursuing my dreams. I knew when I was 17 years old that I would not be afraid of what everyone else was, and I would share my life with the world, hoping they would still love me. I still remember the first days of living in LA; we immediately encountered some tough emotional times, but we made it through. When I was still in my U-Haul truck with all my stuff, I let a car pass me as it crossed into the gas station. There was one more lane of traffic that I was blocking the view of the person, not by choice. I was being nice and letting them pass. Yes, a car came and hit them as they were pulling into the gas station. I was like, "This is so

LA. I've got to watch my back. Anything can happen here in LA." Shortly after that, I pull up to her house deep in Benedict Canyon. We have four major events that come up quickly and do not go as planned; Jesus, that was crazy. I am not sure I would have done the same thing if the roles were reversed.

I believe her birthday was the first significant event that arose, and I was very much trying to climb the social ladder when I first arrived. She had a birthday party at her house for her close friends, and about 25 to 40 people attended. Everyone had heard that she let me move in, and they were all curious to see who I was and what I was like. I had haters even before I had a chance to give them a good reason to hate me. Little did I know how envious some of these people were of me. I was slightly embarrassed to be in this position, and I did not know how to act my age. I try to maintain my youthful spirit as much as possible. I don't give a fuck about my age; I care about my reflection in the mirror. I care about how much money I can blow on my friends and what I can share with my loved ones. So, at this party, we were all drinking and having a good time. Her sister was there, and she was a low-key hater for a long time. As the night progressed, most of the people started to leave, and we found ourselves in the master bedroom. For some reason, we started to get sexual. There was an older lady who was a lesbian for the last 15 years, and she was somehow involved with us. I was in and out of a black out, and new pussy always has an alluring nature to me. She was not attractive to me at all. I was nervous just let the spirit take over that night.

I was distracted and left to go get a bottle of Krug that was 20 years old. I knew it was the best of the choices. When I get

100

drunk, I become an entertainer, and I strive to create the most entertaining situation possible. What ended up happening was I had sex with this lesbian who was like 50 years old from an established family in Beverly Hills, and my birthday girl was mad, and she left with the bottle of Krug. I woke up the next morning wondering what had happened. I had just moved in, and I think she wanted to keep what happened a secret from everybody because I'm sure that was the last thing she had expected to happen. This night would come back to haunt her for many days, and this was just the beginning. It was a good thing I had made it at this time, as the maid was able to clean the whole house and make everyone breakfast in the morning. I was a bit surprised that everything seemed to be kosher; we were making plans for a little family vacation to Hawaii. She must have promised her daughter that she would take everyone to Hawaii for summer vacation. I'm sure for the longest time, the mom felt like she got the raw end of the stick, and her new baby girl, 16, was getting the silver spoon treatment her whole life. So, it was time for her mom to have a young guy to share her life with and live it up.

She gave her daughter the French benefits of privilege, and so it was only fair that her mom could have some fun too. I was catching the tail end of the fun here; most of the wealth was blown away by her ex-husband, who was a wild soul. Eight hundred thousand dollars was, let's say, taken from her and spent wastefully, leaving a really bad taste in the family's mouth. They did not trust anyone, especially her sister. This cut off what I felt I deserved, but anything was better than living in Idaho. So, I accepted having almost none of the same privileges that one should have for playing the lead male in this mix. I was unaware of any of this at the time. There was a family dynamic; the mom is 43, and I am 30. My daughter is 16. We are all about a decade and a half apart from each other. Although I am the young blood, I don't like old people's shit. So, mom would get pissed when the daughter and I agreed on shit like music to listen to, which was really sad and funny at the same time. Additionally, the pecking order is as follows: the daughter takes precedence most of the time, unless she's on her mom's nerves; next comes the mom; and then comes the sister. I was fourth and least important because of my actions, probably, and the ex-husband was worse than Kevin. She had a baby daddy, which was another story, too. I was essentially a boy toy for the most part, which came with some privileges and also some responsibilities. This reminded us both of the movie spread that Ashton Kutcher was in, and he lived just up the street from us at the time.

At that time, the iPhone 4S was just being released, on October 4, 2011, when we landed in the Hawaiian Islands. She got me the new iPhone 4, and this is when I started filming my life in LA. She decided to rent out a condo for the days that we were there. This was dope because we went to the store and spent around $500 on food and drinks for the house. It was a trip just because we could. So, this was where I could really bond with the daughter and her boyfriend at the time, so that they could get a feel for me, and it wasn't weird having me in the house. It's a big decision for Mom to let me into the house. We all had a great time in Hawaii. We had plenty of dinners out at the town's fanciest restaurants. The first guy I asked to get some Maui Wowie was able to get it so we had bomb ass weed too. Now I'm still tripping because, at the end of the night, I had to go to bed with Mom. This bitch wanted dick all the time. I told her I need Viagra to hit, and she was like, "Okay, I got it. Take it."

I was like, "Oh shit." She knew that she wasn't my first choice, and she knew that I was in a tough position, and I was live meat in the cougar's den. This was better than old school SF bull shit. It was real money and real life with no chance of breaking any laws. I'm not selling drugs or pimping or holding guns to people's heads. I am in a cougar's den, and she wants to feel me. So, I was like fuck it. I swallowed the pill and took care of business. She reminded me that the whole time in bed, I hadn't kissed her once. She even said, "How are you going to fuck me without the pleasure of a kiss?" I fucking lost it. I was like, "What the fuck is going on? I'm out."

This woman had me trippy—I was barely dressed and still high from the weed—she had me so upset that I stormed out of the house, heading anywhere but where she was. We had been loud and fighting, which woke up her daughter. Thankfully, she was kind enough to chase after me and convince me that if I left the house in that state, I was going to end up in jail. The rest of the night was pretty cloudy; I'm fairly certain I just passed out.

The next day, it was not something we talked about; they were already masters of disillusion, and they moved on to make it pleasant again. I was like, "What the fuck? Just go with the flow; it's not that bad." Everyone was aware of what was happening and the situation. Later that evening, we were going to play beer pong. The teams were Mom versus Daughter. Mom wanted to drink champagne, so we had champagne on our side and beer on the other side. One whole bottle was poured onto our side, and in less than 20 minutes, the game was over. I thought it would be a good idea to put Patron in the middle of each side, so we did that, and we both ended up being hammered. I don't remember how that night ended; that was pretty much how our trip was going. We moved to the next hotel, and things got a little better, calmer, and chill. I do remember losing my brand-new phone at this one hotel party. I got drunk really quickly and thought it was funny to pull the top down to this really old lady in the pool, and we left fairly quickly after that. So, I forget that when I'm in party mode, I think whoever ever around me is also in party mode. I get the reality mixed up with the dream world in my own head. That's what happened with the random lady in the pool. Confusion! Next, we were flying home to Beverly Hills. The funny thing is that the vacation wasn't as nice as being home in Beverly Hills.

That's the first time in my life that home was better than vacation. After all that crazy time, we got me a new phone when we got back, and I was in awe of the craziness we experienced. She just let it pass. I was living in LA LA Land. She gave me the S500 to drive around, and she signed me up for club sport in Beverly Hills, so that I could work out. I had these two girls I loved so much who were just becoming baby porn stars, Riley Jensin and Sara James. These girls had all my love at the time. I told them what I was doing with this cougar in Beverly Hills, and they thought it was dope. She was like, "How did you get her to let you have the Benz?" I was like, "She just said, 'Here are the keys.'"

So, these girls were 19 and 20 years old. I had 23 years between the girls I was fucking with and the cougar I was living with. I figured it was a worthwhile trade, being able to have a fantasy life on both sides.

I was just lacking the skills to make my own money. This is the devil's dream to make you believe you have life because it's all around you, but it does not belong to you. These girls were young hustlers, and it was always a pleasure to fuck with them. They were getting paid thousands of dollars to eat each other's pussies on camera. I told her she was going to be as famous as Kacey Jordan because she embodies that teenager fantasy girl. We loved doing cocaine together and getting fucked up. The day she told me that she was flying to Mexico with Kacey Jordan and they were shooting scenes together, I was like, "Fuck yeah." I knew this shit was going to happen. I had my brother on the other side, who was living with the Packard Street Boys, a clique he created. I would deal with life on the West Side; then I would move to the East Side. It was a balance of epic proportions for me. I found a job doing hair extensions for one of the best friends of the lady I was living with; it turns out that we met in Northern California because my mom had bought me Bio Ionic tools, and she worked for Bio Ionic in LA, and she was at the trade show in San Jose.

So, she recommended that I work for them, and I was able to shoot a commercial for them in Beverly Hills, which looked fantastic. I was very excited to be part of this team. Bio Ionic asked me to be an Educator for them, and I was able to travel around the country doing hair shows. My dreams started to come true in LA. When I was a kid, my brothers had me steal these adult magazines because I was very young, and they said that the people wouldn't notice me taking them, so I became good at it. This was the beginning of my addiction to girls who didn't mind being naked. I love naked girls and everything about open sexual life.

Love is sex to me, and love is friendship. Connection is sex to me; it's intimacy, it's our bodies feeling each other. So, to live in LA, where all the sexist girls live, I was in dreamland. Sara and Riley introduced me to Ash Hollywood and this girl Nina James. I loved all these girls; they were just like me, and they wanted to party and fuck and make money and hustle. It's fucked up because the world will judge you on how you live your life. My past left me damaged, and I couldn't see any future; my focus was solely on fun. I often thought, when it's over, I'll just die. This isn't the best way to think or live. My fantasies were becoming reality, and I love pretty girls; it's my nature, and it's the most powerful thing in the world to me at this point in my life.

I felt like the older people in life took my youth from me and gave me money, cars, and a college education. Life is about trading time for the things your parents can't give you. We are sexual beings, and when sex in your life stops, we become dried-up and boring people, so I thought. When the secret gets out that we are sexual beings, the world will possibly hold it against you, or in Kim Kardashian's case, it will make you famous beyond belief. So, this is my dilemma. I am torn and I am stuck. The lady who let me move in with her in Beverly Hills. Here is the rest of the story. We took a trip to Montecito to rekindle our connection. Living in Beverly Hills with her has been a wild ride, and this was a way for us to really see what our future was. When it's just us two, we are fine, and we get to relax and have fun, and we see eye to eye. That means we're good to keep going. She had an SLS Mercedes, which we got from LA to Montecito in about 90 minutes; I was driving fast. So, we get to have a relaxing weekend. The next big event is her daughter's birthday, so she asks me what we should do. I was like, "Let's get a stretched limo and take her to a fancy dinner with all her friends and have a house party after."

That was all approved, and we did it. I had a few of my male model friends come through, and the daughter and her friends were like, "Wow."

I was like, "No, you cannot!!"

We all got to party, and everything was good in the house. We have to remain calm; it's no big deal. The house came with two pets: Starlet, a lucky kitty, along with a dog that was really cute to have named Lucky. I was in love with the cat; he was my best friend when things got weird at the house. One night, we drove up to Beverly Glen to get dinner, and I was at the wheel. I pulled over to look at the sunset and smoke a cigarette, as we were in the convertible. I closed the door on my thumb, and this was the worst pain I had ever experienced in my life. I suffered all night long. She would give me tequila to calm the pain, and I had to go to the doctor in the morning and have them laser a hole in my nail to release the pressure. My nail fell off; it was a traumatic experience. I knew I wasn't living life the right way, and I wanted to escape this lifestyle, but I had no way out. I had no way of earning my own living and achieving the true success I had always dreamed of. I was just going from one party to the next party and being a bad ass that had no rules to live by. Waking up empty, I was free as a bird, with hopes and dreams.

I was searching for love and success, but I couldn't find true love or financial freedom. I was becoming depressed and hopeless; I had booked a couple of modeling jobs that would pay like $500, one for this Italian swimsuit company. This would bring me a little hope; meanwhile, as my other friends were booking high-paying jobs, $ 1,500 runway shows, and TV commercials. The one stripper girlfriend that introduced me to the lady I am living with in Beverly Hills was moving to LA, and we spent some time together. We had partied and had a threesome.

I was proud of myself for taking the girls to my friend's house, but my male friends weren't impressed with the girls because they weren't models. I started to feel like I wasn't as good as my close friends, and I realized that real modeling wasn't for me. Due to my appearance, I wasn't in demand, and I didn't feel white enough for mainstream modeling or acting. Maybe if I had green eyes or was friends with Jennifer Lopez. This was a tough pill to swallow, as my dreams all included me landing big-time acting jobs. I started to party more and go out on the weekends, just like always. Old Lady, she would get jealous of me being out and call me nonstop, asking me to come home, even though she said she didn't mind me going out.

After meeting hundreds of pretty girls, I still hadn't connected with anyone on a solid level where I could feel love. We had a job to do in New York City around the beginning of

October 2010. So, we flew to NYC, and every time we would go out, I would always end up meeting some younger, prettier girls and taking pictures with them. All I really wanted was one good girl to fall in love with; it's just that she would have to have lots of money because I had none. I guess the old lady was it. I continued to feel doubt, and what felt like LA didn't choose me like it chose 2Pac. I felt a little pleasure from our life together, traveling and seeing New York City. We took a horse and carriage through the park, and she was mad that I wasn't really into it. Sara and Riley happened to be in NYC at the same time I was, so we were excited, and we got to hit Times Square for a little while, take pictures, and I was so happy with both of them. All I wanted was to be in love with one of my favorite beautiful girls. My old lady is in a situation where she has achieved all her dreams at work and with money, and she wants a young guy like me to fall in love with her. We talked about this, and I told her I was willing to be her friend, but I couldn't fall in love with her. All the men who fell in love with her, she could not stand, even though they had all the money it took to impress her with parties and black cards; she wanted me. I remember once pocket dialing her from my cell phone, and I was with all my boys in her S500, explaining the details of how I felt about her. She was pretty upset and crying. This was in LA.

So, I had asked one of my model friends to have sex with her, as all my other young girls wanted to fuck him. I thought she would too. She told me she didn't want that. Even though we had a plan and he was at the house trying to fuck her. I think he wanted to have her in his back pocket as a backup plan. He was a legit Abercrombie model and a complete white boy from Colorado. I was shocked that she did not take the bait. I flew to visit my family in Idaho and got to see what life was like out there. We shot guns and spent quality time with family. Both of my brothers were living up there, and my mom was happy to see me. I had started to grow accustomed to my lifestyle in Beverly Hills. I was happy to be living in California; still, this was where my dreams were slowly slipping in and out of reality. When I came back, it was straight back to the nightlife and parties. One day, I was lucky enough to run into Jermaine Dupri and Too Short on the same day, and I was able to take pictures with both of them. Little things like this made me feel like a budding young celebrity in LA. I met Asher from Asher Entertainment at a fashion show after-party in Beverly Hills, and he hired me to style the hair of his dancers for events in Orange County on New Year's. I loved working freelance jobs; it's exciting to work with talented dancers. This was the life I should have continued building, and I did because I respected the work, and I was happy doing hair for these events.

We had a wonderful Thanksgiving at home in LA, and everything was pleasant and enjoyable. Soon, I began to find more and more friends from San Francisco who were moving to LA. I have pictures of good friends all out at the parties in Hollywood. I began to understand how the nightlife industry operates in LA. Then, a really cool job opportunity arose just before Christmas. It was the Mercedes-Benz Christmas party in Huntington Beach, and I had the opportunity to style the dancers' hair again for Asher Entertainment. I was finding success and making good friends who could enjoy my work. I met Emily that day, who also worked for a club in Hollywood called Playhouse. Emily had me come in a week later to style hair for one of the events at Play House, and I felt like my career was starting to take shape. Christmas in Beverly Hills arrives, and we all enjoy a wonderful holiday season filled with good times. We began to find some balance, and we were good friends with slight benefits, which started to feel normal. I still wanted to escape secretly. I was meeting all sorts of beautiful girls all over the country and it was my fantasy surrounded me and when I would come home alone I would look at what my friends were doing in the XXX world and I felt like I would rather get paid to have sex with 18-19-year-old girls than be forced to have sex with this older one. I knew it could be career suicide, but I was so deep in bullshit that I had to live out the fantasy. I had to take the risk.

The tattoo on my balls seemed like a good reason to become famous, and so I signed the contract I had been holding onto from LA Direct. I thought if I had to change my name to a new one for a hair salon that wouldn't even let me take a honeymoon, had I been married, I could use that same name to fulfill my sexual fantasies. I had already had to deal with gay San Francisco, and this was my chance to live out my childhood fantasies with women I thought were very sexy. How many men get the chance to live this life? After hosting numerous bachelorette parties, why not try this? I figured I might gain enough acting experience to create a real reel, maybe together, and who knows what could happen? It's different for men, right? I didn't want to be this man, living in Beverly Hills with this older cougar. I felt at home with the strippers and the bad girls. They were all okay with me as I was a treasure to them. They had to deal with the ugly, old rich men, while I was a good-hearted man just hoping to become famous enough to make a difference in this world. How many people will read my story, and will this hit a chord with young people growing up in today's world? Will this story become a movie?

2011 LA

I spent the new year with my best friends in Hollywood, and I met the girl who would take me out of Beverly Hills by random chance in the future. She was a beautiful red-headed girl who came from a good family. We just met that night and exchanged information, and took some pictures. The next day, my boys and I went to Santa Monica to have lunch and just relax. I met one of my good friends, who is a spiritual advisor to me, and she was a free spirit, able to help me understand all the emotional craziness happening in my life. I felt like I needed to get out of Beverly Hills and be on my own. I had hopes and dreams of being a celebrity, which comes with risks. I felt like Hollywood was unfair to Latinos and Asians, and I was willing to do whatever it takes to become famous to be a voice, so wherever I needed to get my start, I was going to start there. My first job was with Alexis Texas, and I was keeping it a secret that I was going to try this world. I had partied all night in the house in Beverly Hills, and we were up late, and I knew I had this job the next day.

She really didn't want me to go; it's like somehow, she knew what I was doing. I was sick and tired of being under her rules, and I really needed to have sex with someone I was attracted to. So, I show up to set at around 9 am and sit and wait until 12 noon. I slept on the couch for a bit, as we were still not shooting. My time was running out to take this shot. She kept calling my cell phone and texting me that she was going to have to sue the person she was working for, who was a major player in the Christian TV scene and got his start with Oprah. She was crying and begging me to come home, but I felt incapable of dealing with the stress from her and this first shoot. I wanted to call my agent and tell him I had to go; I freaked out and just left the set. They had to call a new guy to come in and do the scene. I got in trouble for sure. I was called in to LA Direct, and Derek said, "Even Charlie Sheen has to call a deal with the BS; you can't just leave the set without telling anyone."

I was like, maybe I should take a break until I can get out of this cougar's house, and I will be free to shoot. They gave me a second chance, and my first scene was with Heather Starlet, which was a simple scene; all she had to do was jack me off. This was my first time appearing on camera, aside from the home videos I shot.

I had made three with my best girlfriends, girls I truly loved. So, this was crazy, having some hot blonde chick get me off I was really excited, and it all went well. This was the kind of break I needed from my home life, which had started to fall apart so quickly that it felt like a tornado of disaster. She was plagued by a series of events that would be worth being featured on E!'s True Hollywood Stories. First, she received a letter of notice to vacate her office on Canon Street in Beverly Hills. These offices were 10k a month. When she lost the support of her celebrity client and all the executives from Paramount, she wasn't able to maintain the office. As I mentioned, I was coming into this as everything was falling apart. I had no idea what I was in for either. On January 18th, we moved out of the office, and I did my best to help her pack up all her belongings and move them into storage. This wasn't an easy day for either of us. I went out that night after it was all done and really fucked up.

It was Dead Mau5's birthday in Hollywood, and I was drinking pretty heavily and wanted to get some blow to wake me up. My friend didn't have it, so he offered me a double stack of E. I was like, "Shit."

I took it, and I was doing better until we got to the after-party. There was a girl at the after-party with whom I was somewhat familiar, and the E made me really aggressive. I was kicked out of the party, and I couldn't just stay in the car. I waited for as long as I could, and this was before I had Uber, and I was embarrassed about being kicked out of the after-party. I just wanted to come home. So I drove home the black Mercedes 100k car, and I ruined the rims on the sides of the car. I had hit this sidewalk in the middle of the road. The city later removed this because it was dangerous. I have to leave the car there and walk home or call a taxi. When I got home, I was emotional, and she took me in and made me feel okay. We fixed the car, and she was able to sell it for $30,000, which she really needed at the time. However, it wasn't how she wanted to see the car leave her life. She told me that the car was a symbol of her "making it." It was the first car she paid cash for, and it was the family car. I felt guilty about it, and I was still immersed in this new dream world that was difficult to take seriously. Even though it was my actual life, I hope you can all gain insights from it.

I was still obsessed with the possibilities and the fantasy that lay ahead of me. Problems that would have set me back years were things that she could overcome in less than 24 hours. Right around this time, I was offered a chance to be on a showtime show called, 'Gigalo's' and my friend Nick Hawk was on the show but I wasn't able to tell the world yet that I was living in a world that my sex was being used to counter balance the scales of misfortune in my life. So I turned down that opportunity.

My best friend was having a birthday on February 4th, and he only had room for four friends. I wasn't able to make it that night, so I borrowed my friend's car, the same one that had been recommended to me to take this wild trip with the lady in Beverly Hills. I clearly remember deciding not to go home that night. I was able to visit this girl's house, whom I was sort of seeing, and she just moved to Santa Monica. She had a girlfriend there, and we just got drunk. Of course, I was interested in both of them, and with some success, we had a great night. To make a long story short, I really dislike this part. The next day, we woke up still partying, yada yada yada. I'm driving home, totally blacked out, and somehow I made it from Santa Monica to Beverly Hills; I was so close to being home. Regardless, I was on a war path with myself; I was destroying myself. I was living a lie with this older woman, and I needed to get out of that, and all the drugs and drinking led me to this DUI. I don't want to write out all the details of this accident.

I let my foot off the brake when the light turned green, and the lady in front of me did not go, so I rolled into her. This was a love tap, but it was bullshit. I was three sheets to the wind and couldn't contain myself. I woke up at the wheel, not even knowing I was there. If I went down Benedict Canyon, I could have killed myself or someone else, and I am so grateful for the way it ended because I learned my lesson. I had to go to jail that day, and I was so mad at myself. I just fucked up my life.

We got an attorney who helped me postpone my trial, and we won the DMV case, allowing me to drive legally until I was proven guilty in a court of law. So, I was able to drive to my freelance job and all the AA meetings I had to attend. Life went on as usual, and in March, I was able to travel to Chicago for the first time with the Bio Ionic team for a huge trade show. When I returned to LA, I was able to purchase my second RX-7. This one was a white one, and I really have a soft spot in my heart for RX7s.

I flew up to the Bay Area because my grandma had passed away. This was the first time I had ever had to experience death in my family. It was really hard for me to feel my feelings, and at first, I was immune to them. Later, it hit me, and I was able to take a few pieces of my childhood with me that I remember from my grandmother's house. I still have them today and use them quite often. I have really moved on from the Bay Area; everything there was stale to me, and I was immersed in the drama of my new life in LA. While I was in the Bay, my mother helped me get a new tattoo, and that's when I got my next blue star on my right arm. When I got back to LA, I started hanging out with my New Year's girl, who would take me out to Beverly Hills. The mounting pressure of all the drama in Beverly Hills would be tearing me apart and adding to the stress she was already experiencing with her own life. She saw me beginning to grow and build a real life in LA, while simultaneously spiraling out of control and crashing two cars in less than 30 days. She knew I hated playing this game of cat and mouse with her.

She could tell that I was a true Gemini; my Venus is in Gemini, and I have multiple faces in my love life. I have the ability to be many different people in love. I am an actor, and I play coy. I evolve and I adapt. I can find your soft spot and massage it to give you the pleasure no one else does. When I need you in life, I will find a way to make myself invaluable to you. As I grow my business, my beautiful, red-haired model girlfriend invites me over to style her hair for her birthday, and we have a great time. Then on March 30th, I came back over to her place to do color and cut, and we ended up drinking and smoking some pot, so I stayed the night with her. That set Beverly Hills ablaze. Following the bachelor pad rules, I was confronted by a crying, angry soul who asked me to move out. This was a dream come true. I was able to find an apartment on March 31st, 2011, which was in less than 24 hours. I moved all my stuff into my own bachelor pad. My rent was less than $1,000. I had a walk-in closet, a separate kitchen, and an office to work in. This place was perfect for me to rebuild my life. It was close to my best friend's house, and it was down the street from my current job at Bio Ionic - walking distance. It was also right across the street from the hair shop on Wilshire, which was a blessing because I made the majority of my money from doing hair extensions.

This was the premier place to buy hair extensions, not to mention that the Wilshire Beauty Supply was right on the corner, where I had all my color needs met. I moved into a huge hub of hair salons by accident. This was a true golden gem to be found in LA. Then I headed to St. Louis for work. I loved flying around the country for work; it was a dream come true. I felt like I had found my calling in life and was finally able to take pride in being a hair stylist. As a 30-year-old, I was making all my dreams come true. I was still partying like a rock star, and that would catch up to me as it always does. I really needed a girlfriend who would commit to me and show me love. I was a wild sex machine with an attraction to so many girls. I wanted to fuck them all. I know that I am telepathic, and I can send you a signal that tells you I want to fuck you with just a glance. A girl will catch the vibe of sexual energy, and this isn't always a good thing in a professional environment.

I knew it, but I wasn't completely aware that this was a reality. I didn't think people were that smart, and the more I realized it, the more I had to control it. I met a Latina girl on Facebook or Instagram, and she messaged me. I really loved her style; she was amazing. Next thing you know, I'm flying off to Iowa and Nebraska for work, and it was quite amazing to see parts of the country I would never visit on my own. I took pride in my work and was employed by an amazing company. However, now that I had to pay my own rent, it was a growing phase. I was ready for it. I felt so happy to have my own place. I had an audition for Wicked Pictures on April 12th, just a day before my birthday. I was pretty excited about the opportunities that could come my way, but then I had my 31st birthday at Colony Night Club, and I met a new girlfriend who was also Latina. Amanda was with me celebrating my birthday, and Amanda has been a close friend for some time. Then I was on some Latin TV show called 12 Corazones's just a very short gig. I met more Latin girls with whom I'd like to stay friends. Shortly after that, my first film was released on the internet, and I got to see myself in it. It wasn't as if I wanted to share it with people I knew, but I was happy to see it. I don't think there is anything wrong with it. I would rather make my money that way than have to live in Beverly Hills. I thought it would be cool to have a sugar momma, but this was torture. I would continue to participate in photo shoots to expand my online presence through my website. I was able to work with a friend of mine from the Bay Area, Sal, who started his own company making amazing bracelets out of crocodile.

La Direct had a party at Supper Club in Hollywood, and it was amazing. Riley, Sara, and Ash from Hollywood were there along with other stars, and I just loved being there. I thought it was a lot of fun. I always wanted to throw my own sex parties all over the world, styling hair and choosing the hottest models to represent the beauty of all cultures. I guess this is validation of my manliness. I followed my heart and let my soul be carefree. I found satisfaction in sexual energy, the release of it. It's a privilege to be able to live out your fantasies without punishment from a God. I met an angel on Model Mayhem who was to be my best friend for some time. She would be my hair model for some shoots, and I would be able to help her find some security. She was not as sexually open as I was, and for a girl to be my girlfriend, I really need her to be as bad as me, and if not, I feel like I am corrupting her, and I really don't want to do that to anyone. I prefer that they already have their own issues when we meet.

I don't want to be the one who pushes them over any edge in life. If you're seeking a new life, I can help you find it. I just can't be your gateway unless I love you, and you become my soulmate. I would never suggest that someone do something I wouldn't do myself; that's just who I am. I was able to put together a group of girls for a photo shoot at the supper club with five of my favorite hot girls. This was the first time I had the opportunity to have a former Playmate model for me. Susan Stokes came through, and we shot a great shoot, and we all went out to eat after. Susan and I would remain close, and I was able to do her extensions for some time, along with those of her other playmate girlfriends, like Buffy Tyler. A phone call came in to shoot the cover of Maxim Magazine with a photographer I had worked with in San Francisco. They needed me to find them a location with a waterfall, and this is how freelance work goes. I knew a friend who lived in Mount Olympus, and I was able to lock down the location for the photographer. The drama was fairly intense during this shoot.

My friend with the house wanted $1200 for the location. The photographer wanted to pay $300, and my friend with the house knew that they would be making good money off the shoot if it was for the cover for Maxim, so he didn't give in until he got $1100. I think if the budget allows for fair pay, you might as well take care of the people working for you. Say he was given a $5,000 budget, and he pays the model $1,000 and $1,100 for the house. How would it be fair that he only paid $3000 for the house? That's not a legit amount. To make things worse, the wind blew over a reflector that broke my friend's vase, so I ended up losing the photographer as a friend.

So, Kayla, the real estate agent, and I started to date, and she had a son who could have been mine, it seemed like. She was also a hair stylist, and she lived in the OC. I just mean like I could have gotten a girl like her pregnant, and she could have been my baby's momma. It felt like I was being shown what life would be like if I were really an adult and had a small family of my own that was just starting. Believe it or not, I do appreciate that. I just really wish that if I were to have my own kids, they would be mine with the woman I love. I suppose I am quite traditional in that regard. I want to stay married when I get married. I really hope that one day I will get married and have a home to move into with a good job; that's my heart's desire. At this time in my life, though, having her son come over and visit with her was not easy for me. I tried to cope with it, and it was just tough. I was very selfish, and I wanted the girl all to myself. So, we eventually drifted apart. However, it is a fond memory. Later in life, I would see her on TV in a famous show. In her First scene, she brought her son with her. I was shocked, but also not.

My hair styling gigs kept coming in. I had a girl from the Bay Area come down to go to the Playboy Mansion, and they wanted me to style their hair, so I did. The next project I worked on took me back to the Playhouse for another gig, where I was building some good contacts. I always specialized in creating really big mohawks. Soft, elegant hair wasn't my thing back then. On July 7th, I styled hair again for a playhouse, and this was a really big shoot that went onto a Billboard for the two-year anniversary. I was so excited to have styled hair that went to a billboard; I really felt like I was on the right path. However, I had this DUI pending, and if I could just keep my license, I would be able to continue doing these gigs and making fair money.

After we shot this, we had the actual party at the Playhouse on the weekend, and I was hired again to do mohawks for all the dancers there. I was working fairly often between all my hustles and clients. It was summertime in LA, and we had pool parties to attend, capturing many good memories on my iPhone. The billboard was up on July 16th. I saw it and took some pictures. Kayla and I were still seeing each other at the time, and we had a wonderful night out on the town. I was still working with Bio Ionic and learning their keratin smooth straightening process. My best friend's brother's girlfriend came in to have me straighten her hair. This was very similar to the Brazilian blowout, although it did not contain formaldehyde, making it a great process. I was building my online portfolio as much as possible, shooting with girls like Caitlyn and Faith. Now that I was living on my own, things were much better in Beverly Hills. As long as the slate was wiped clean, we were all good to party. I would continue to work for her as she needed her taxes done for her lawsuit against a celebrity talk show host.

I was really using her to go to the tabloids and leak her private information because he was really screwing her over; she had almost died because of his advice. Now, part of me really loved her and her family, and I still do. As I write about it, I want you to know that I am eternally grateful for all the good times we shared in love. As I continue to tell the story, you will see where it gets worse. My friend Riley had her 21st birthday on a huge boat in Marina Del Ray, and it was a very expensive celebration. I am still pretty amazed at how well she put this together. She had rappers show up and perform. We had a fashion show, a gambling event, and it was a white party. I would estimate that about 200 private guests attended. The whole thing was filmed with a red-carpet entrance. It was an amazing time. You will have to see the footage. Pretty much all of my LA trip has been recorded, so you can see all the footage that I can legally post. Fast forward, and parties keep happening one after another.

The next cool job I styled hair for was the producer of "Friday." A birthday party was held at the Mr. C hotel in Beverly Hills, organized by Asher Entertainment. We had little people and dancers; everyone was dressed up, wearing white python snakes. I was able to join the party and see a few celebrities, including Ice Cube and Jamie Foxx, among others.

I took a road trip to San Diego with Enzo Milano to work at a hair show at the San Diego Convention Center. I was able to find my Play House billboard ad in a local magazine that I kept a few copies of for sweet memories. I met a girl named Shelby, who became a friend, and later she appeared in my life in Los Angeles. She also made an appearance on TV, starring in "The Plastic Cup Boys," a production by Kevin Hart. 2011 was moving along pretty quickly. In October, I did a shoot with Faith, where I built a bird cage in her hair with a swing and used a real Parakeet for a super unique couture look. I was still attending 3 AA meetings a week to satisfy the court for my DUI. It's eye-opening to learn how many people in LA struggle with drinking and how, when they quit, some are able to find real success. I never made any real friends in AA. Everyone was too cool for school, or just seemed to close off to really any fun. I met a friend, whom I won't name, who is Russian and came to LA to pursue a career as an actor or singer. We both missed drinking, so we decided to go out and have a drink.

I was able to return home at a reasonable time and continue my life as usual. The week continued to progress, and

I started wondering where my friend was and why he wasn't answering his phone or coming to meetings. So, I went over to his house and found him at home. He had continued to drink nonstop since the day we started. He had nearly 200 cans of beer next to him, all empty. They were scattered around his apartment, all around the bed; it was a mess. We decided to take him to Cedar's Hospital and help him detox. He had given himself delirium tremors. This is when I realized I am not a true alcoholic; I am a drinker who has problems. I always have someone to bail me out, pay my rent, or help me get back on track. Because I made friends with people who wanted to have me in their lives, they would be willing to keep me from feeling bad about my drinking; they would say, "Don't beat yourself up." They would take me out to eat and have some fun all on their dime. So, I never needed to make my own money.

Until I realized that I wasn't having fun anymore, I needed to stand on my own two feet and make real money, not just barely survive. I wanted to experience true freedom, achieve the American dream, and have a beautiful girlfriend who truly loves and respects me. I can't let older people pay for me; I want to build my own fortune and make all my own decisions. I have all these beautiful girls who are my friends, but they all want a man who is rich, lives in the hills, and has multiple cars, who can buy them shoes and any little desire they have. At this point in my life, I am chasing a dream that is just out of my reach. I am being cast in xxx movies. When I was young as a kid all I ever wanted was to have sex with the girls in the movies, and I am. I was cast in a parody of Final Destination with Asphyxia Nior. We shot downtown LA. We got to dress up and act like we were killed with blood everywhere. This was pretty fun.

Later in life, she would come into my life and live out a fantasy. When I was leaving the set, I got her number, and I was walking to my car, still in costume & blood everywhere, and the homeless people in downtown LA were feeling bad for me, thinking I was really bleeding and hurt. I next shot for Penthouse, and this was shot in 3D. It was really crazy. They had a great set, with everything top-of-the-line for this industry. The model I was working with used to be a runway model; however, I wasn't ready for this: lights, camera, action.

The lighting made the room hot. When she was blowing me, she was making all these hardcore sounds that were an act, and it just threw me off; it didn't feel real. I remember closing my eyes on set, then opening them, and my consciousness was telling me, "What the fuck are we doing here? How is this a job? How the fuck am I here right now?"

Then I was enjoying myself, and I could feel the pleasure of sex, and I was in a blissful state. This was the big time; I had to perform and give it my all. The producers are like, "Okay, it's time to cum. Make sure to cum on her lips."

After our scene was complete, we all sat down and ate at Chipotle. They had ordered us lunch, which was a normal thing. To me, it was a very corporate thing; it was my first, and looking back, it was pretty crazy. I wish we had the option to choose our partners in this business; it's strange to me that we don't. I never got to see this shoot; maybe one way I will. Halloween is right around the corner, and the Porn Industry party was in Hollywood. I dressed up as a cowboy in all black and shirtless. That night was pretty cool. I was with one of my close girlfriends, who was also a porn star, and was dating a producer. We partied with four young starlets who were only doing solo and girl-girl scenes. Those four girls would go on to become pretty major porn stars, the biggest one being Riley Reid.

We all went over to the after party, and that's where I met the prettiest girl, Malena Morgan, who got to shoot with all my girlfriends. These girls were doing very well for themselves at the time for their age. I was booked shortly after shooting for a reality porn company. They gave us the freedom to hold our own camera and make it seem real, within guidelines. It was a bachelorette party, which I was already familiar with. They had told us which girls were blood tested and able to have sex with, and what girls were just extras on set to make it look like a real party. That shoot was pretty intense; we were dressed and able to just freely have an orgy. I didn't mind that other people were in the room; I didn't know anyone, and it was just a big sexual fantasy. People were a lot more welcoming than in real life, like this would never just happen at a party. I was able to have sex with four different girls that day and cum multiple times. It was incredible. I never saw that footage either. I would meet girls on set as an extra and have them come over to my place and do a photo shoot with them for fun. I would style their hair, and we all were willing to just fuck each other a few times. That's why everyone in LA is single; sex can be everywhere with anyone who's willing to meet up with you. I still had a real agent in LA for mainstream modeling jobs that I did not tell I was shooting XXX.

I was booked on a shoot for a skin wax company, and I am naturally pretty hairless. They wanted me for my abs. For some reason, I never really felt beautiful when I was on set for normal modeling jobs. I had emotional insecurities. I wish I could look the camera straight in the eye and just feel beautiful. I smile from the heart when I have a girlfriend by my side, and I'm happy to be with her, or when I feel like I'm in love. During all of these sexual adventures, I grew further and further away from reality. I was always living in a dream world where these things didn't really happen to normal people. I felt special, but still, the money wasn't there. When I have hundreds of thousands of dollars in the bank, that's when I will feel truly special. All these shoots and sex didn't make me wealthy, and I was left emptier. I guess the money would allow me to travel and be carefree. I could go to Japan or Paris and just live there for six months. Having lots of money would give me confidence and freedom as a safety net. I would always come home to just my own studio apartment. I fall in love at first sight, and I truly always want to be in love with just one girl. It's just so hard for me to make that relationship a reality. I always feel like I have too many secrets and too many bad qualities for anyone to ever love me. I find myself with girls who I know are living in the sex industry. Strippers, cam girls, escorts, porn stars, club girls, it's normal to drink and do cocaine, be up all night, and go to raves in Vegas, living the fast life. Those are the girls I feel comfortable with. Normal girls want a family that takes a good job and $300k a year. If you find a pretty normal girl living in LA, she will have high demands. A pretty girl who just moved from the Bible Belt of America may be humble and just right. Will I ever meet a girl who is "normal and humble"? Will I ever have a high-paying job that's $300k?

It's a hole that only falls deeper and deeper into nothingness. Most of us don't know how to take control of our lives. We lack education and the focus to really start a business and live a life that we truly want to live. At times, we have the most fun and adventure, and freedom to be happy and feel beautiful. As the year is ending, the lady in Beverly Hills went to the tabloids to share her story with the world about this dog bite case. Nothing really came of it; I think she was paid to tell the story, but it didn't unfold as I had thought it would. Christmas was right around the corner, and the year was coming to a close. I would spend Christmas Eve with one of my girlfriends who was a playmate. I would drive down to Costa Mesa for the annual New Year's party with Asher, which features entertainment, and I was the hair stylist for the event. Then I would drive back up to LA to spend New Year's with my brother and my club friends at this huge mansion party.

2012 LA

This is the year the Mayan Calendar ends; the world is supposed to end. Lol, spoiler alert: it doesn't. For me, I am getting used to having this LA life. Some days, I'm styling hair; some days, I'm on set having sex with porn stars. I thought I was living a dream life at the time, and I was very happy with my lifestyle. I was working a lot with Brazzers, and Rachel Roxx was a girl I really liked; she would be on set when I was an extra. I also got to meet this one red-headed girl, whom I really liked too. It's a trip to see these girls in real life. I'm sure a lot of men would love to meet their fav porn stars. I feel like sex is just sex. People need to relax a bit and feel happy and loved. That's what this world is all about: sharing love, making your dreams come true, to living in a world where you get to live out your fantasies.

Later, I was booked on another reality shoot. I was to pretend that I was just walking down the street when Heather Starlet came up to me on the street and just asked me if I was down to have sex with her. Now, she was my first girl I ever worked with, and in that shoot, all she did was jack me off. During round 2, I get to have sex with her finally, so I am stoked. She's a hot blonde girl with a really pretty face, and she loves sex, expressing no shame about it.

I got to act a little bit in these films. I had given up on ever shooting a major motion picture, because the game to get in is so hard. I needed to make my own opportunities in this world. Although now, I have dreams of turning my life story into a major motion picture. So the truth about having sex with

Heather was amazing. We were shooting in what looked like a church, and I know it was a bad thing to do so, but her pussy was so tight. I was surprised by her performances. I thought I was less sexually active because she had so much sex drive. This girl's pussy was so tight that I was able to live out my dream with her.

Looking back, I smile at the memory I made that day. I always loved sex and, more than that, money. As I was getting older, I needed to make mounds of money and live the creative life I always dreamt of. I saw myself as a young Andy Warhol, and I needed to have my own studio to create creative ideas. I needed money and cameras, as well as the ability to hire actors and become a legend with my creativity.

As January was ending, I took a trip to the Long Beach Hair Show with Enzo Milano. I got to meet so many cool people at the hair show. I always wondered why LA doesn't have bigger hair shows. It's LA, and we needed a bigger Fashion Week and for it to be more like NYC. Part of my payment was that I was able to choose three styling tools from the Enzo line, and I still use them today.

My confidence was growing, and I felt the blessings of living in a city like LA. I still had that DUI hanging over my head, for which I used to attend three AA meetings per week. My court date also continued to get pushed back further, which meant that I had to keep a good rapport with the Lady in Beverly Hills.

During the beginning of February, when I was still building my portfolio, I got the opportunity to shoot with a beautiful Russian girl in Los Feliz, and she was amazing. I was then asked to do hairstyling at the Playboy Mansion, for which I was so excited to be able to go. This was for Vodka Companies Belvedere's annual party, which was an exclusive black-tie event. This was the only time I would be invited to the Playboy Mansion. This was very cool for me. Like I said, I make my dreams come true. I have had so many of my girlfriends who were able to go there, and it's a shame that it's so hard to be invited if you are a male.

Later that month, my first video with a black girl came out, and I felt like I knew. I have no racial barriers in my life. I loved all types of people and all nationalities. I've let go of any fears regarding sex and color of skin, which allowed me to be fully present whenever I choose my mate in the future.

The next big deal happened at the end of February 2012. I was invited for the first time to appear on the WB network and on the Ellen DeGeneres show on TV. I was to be awarded on a national broadcasting show, and that was another dream coming true! My booker from San Francisco Stripping company called me, asking if I would be able to dance on her show. I felt like I was a little out of shape. Although I was still in shape, I always thought I could do better. I was to be paid to come out dancing with another performer for about a minute and a half when Ellen sprays this new perfume called Billion Dollar Boyfriend, and we come out, surprising the guests of her show, who are attracted by the perfume's smell. It was a blast, and I felt so excited that I was able to be recognized for being a free spirit and be willing to be half-naked on the Ellen Show. The show aired the next day, and I felt so lucky to have that success, even though it didn't pay as a national and commercial TV show.

A few days later, on March 3rd, I am on a plane to Chicago for a hair show with Enzo Milano. This was my second time to Chicago, and it was incredible to be able to travel and charge fees like a superstar. On March 9th, I was styling hair for the LA fashion week. It was a great way to keep myself in the mix as a hair stylist. It gave me a bit of respect, where even some of my girlfriends were models in the shows. The show didn't pay me, and it sucked because I wanted to continue to style hair for shows, but the motivation wasn't there. It was so much work trying to meet their needs, even though we are the ones not getting paid for it. I was hungry and willing to work hard to build a name for myself.

At that point in my life, I felt like I was giving 150% of my energy to find success, but I had yet to gain any meaningful life experiences or financial gain. I was struggling to make ends meet. I sold my skills all over the place, but I barely had anything to show for it. I had stories to tell, along with pictures and videos on my iPhone, to serve as memories.

March's end was coming around when I met the most beautiful Indian girl who came to my house to let me style her hair. I was learning that beautiful girls would let me style their hair, which was a great way to make friends. Styling hair for people doesn't always make them fall in love with me. Usually, I asked the girls with whom I was interested to be in a relationship with to style their hair for free. These girls wanted men who had millions of dollars to fly them around the world, and they really had men who were willing to do this for them.

It was tough to compete with those millionaires, as I was just a man with scissors and a blow dryer, with a fading acting/modeling career. Who am I? Who are they? And what are we doing?... just living the supposed dream life in LA.

I met my friend Jane, who became a really close friend. I told her that I was missing homemade cookies. She said she would be willing to make them with me. So I was able to come to her house, and we made cookies. Later in life, she was able to book me on a few, but really cool, hair styling gigs.

In one of them, there was this club called Beachers Mad House, just opened at the Roosevelt Hotel in Hollywood. I was able to find a way that night. I was able to make a few dreams come true that night. Like how I was able to meet Paris Hilton and take a picture with her, her sister Nikki was there too. My friend Shelby was there from SD at a housewarming party on the west side. My porn friend had some girls over. I was able to become better friends with Malena Morgan, who was smoking and talking about her new movie that was coming out. Little did I know about all the money surrounding her life. Being me with no guidance, I was hopelessly out of the game until I could figure out how to capitalize on the fame game LA has to offer.

I started working for a company called Zen Arts. They were shooting pictures for their website launch. I showed up and created some cool shots with them. This partnership could have lasted longer if the owner of the company hadn't had the habit of hitting on the girls who work for him.

As a hair stylist, I used to talk about everything with the girls until I met this cougar girl who was an artist. She dropped my name in the process when she was dating him, and he fired me from the upcoming shows he had, including EDC and Vegas. She really fucked me over. All I did was pass on the truth about him.

At this point, I don't really care about what people say about me, and I never really hear what people say about me. Nobody ever says anything to my face. I think all my movies are a secret still, and they very well could be. I just don't see how it's a bad thing. Just because I like to have sex, how can people hate me for that? I guess I often forget about religion and the rules they have, as I don't feel that religion has any power over my life. I could discuss my beliefs about how the world truly started with the ancient Sumarians.

Anyhow, the lady in Beverly Hills wanted to take us out, so we went to the Bel Air Hotel for dinner. I was able to take my best friend with me on that dinner too. This whole lifestyle was pretty crazy. I felt like I was living a dream life that wasn't real. Even though it wasn't filled with billionaires and flights to Paris, London, and Tokyo. I was living my simple American dream in California.

I had another shoot in Malibu at this Mansion, which would end in March and bring me into April; my birthday month. I was depressed and lonely on my birthday. I had friends, but I didn't have love. I had big cities, big networks, and parties to go to, but I always came home to being alone. This loneliness was slowly destroying my hopes and dreams. I felt like I had nothing and was nothing. I missed Amber, the love and life I had with her. I felt like I needed a girl who could satisfy me with her love, and then I could go after money, with her by my side. Why does this world want to take my dreams from me and prevent me from achieving true success? I felt so blue on my birthday. Turning 32 made me feel old; I needed my own house in Beverly Hills and a career job that pays $500k. What was I doing? I don't have kids, and I live in my own studio apartment.

The movie "Dirty Love" with Jenny McCarthy came out, and I loved it. She wrote, produced, and starred in it. I admired her, and she was willing to bare it all to become famous and successful. It's just that she became Playmate of the Year, and she was a beautiful blonde girl with green eyes. I was a half-breed Mexican male who had less than $3k to my name, had a bad credit score, was estranged from my family, alone, and lost in a city where my soul is being sold by my agents, from which I'm making pennies. I'm a model from LA Direct, not Wilhelmina, and I have an old cougar in Beverly Hills, who's manipulating my life, wanting to make me act like her husband should.

My escape is that I have the privilege of flying to Vegas to shoot with Riley Reid and then flying back the same day to make it to a High School Graduation party. Keeping all that a secret, of course, I feel ashamed to be part of the family in Beverly Hills. I shouldn't be there; the age gap is too great, and she is not someone I am attracted to. Besides the success, she was able to cultivate in her life. She taught me a thing or two about how money works and all the problems she encountered with having money. I have this huge crush on Veronica, a fellow actress, and I just wish that I could meet her and build a friendship to start a business.

I needed a bit of luck in my life, and I needed a partner. The girls seem to be able to make 10k in one day, which is so crazy! How can this be possible for them to make so much money in just one day? If I could do that, I would be rich and have saved my money, creating an inspiration for the world, because that's what I love. I wanted to be an artist who developed ways of communication that become unforgettable over time.

June was approaching, and I was finally able to get my friend Nikki to join me for lunch in Beverly Hills. I was in love with this girl and wanted to make her my girlfriend, so it was worth taking her out to Beverly Hills. We were on Rodeo Drive at the restaurant above Tiffany's. I don't think she ever saw us as potential lovers. It's possible, but I was just uncomfortable and wanted each girl to know the truth about me. I wanted girls to love me the way I love them, and I don't think I was able to succeed.

I was letting my hair grow long as it was a goal of mine to have long hair. Maybe one way, I will let it all grow again. I was getting into mixing my own music on GarageBand and had dreams of being a DJ. I created music that I still love and listen to today. I was involved in a lawsuit with a clothing company; I think I mentioned it earlier. On June 27th, I signed more paperwork, stating that I would be a proud class representative, which could have put me at risk if we lost the case.

Summer was in full swing, and I had a few girlfriends come in and out of my life. Amber even came to visit with her little dog, Daisy, who was adorable. We just could never have that same spark as we did before. My girl Alice came to visit as well and lived with me for a couple of weeks. I finally started working a normal job and ended everything with the lady in Beverly Hills.

I started working for Planet Beauty, where I earned around $13 per hour and was fully committed to being a good worker. I almost started dating one of the managers from another store. Anytime I start drinking and I find a girl attractive, I go for it. That's why drinking brings out the devil in me. This girl, Skylar, showed up at one of the parties I was at, and she became my true love. She was everything I wanted in a girl. We still talk to this day, but I think she's waiting for me to become successful because she deserves a prince to provide and share the world with. Why can't she just love me now?

September was coming around, and I started working with J Beverly Hills. I did it because I wanted to get back to traveling and being an educator. I started by taking a week-long class to learn about all the organic products they offer. After the week, we were all surprised with a trip to Malibu. The class included a diverse group of people from around the world who had already purchased the products for their salons. There were people from Sweden, and we took a stretched limo to Paradise Cove. We had a great dinner and drank, and I met one of the girls. We sort of fell in love on the beach that night. Of course, I got in trouble for this, as we were told not to spend any time with anyone outside of the class. Of course, I did that; I took her out in Hollywood and showed her a great time in LA. I took a class in Pasadena with J Beverly Hills. Their next big event was in Hollywood on September 30th, and they had their big world tour and shows planned. We had lots of models, and

I was able to bring this girl I was in love with, named Tobi, who was also a hair stylist. But she thought of as a friend and later got married. Fuck, I lost another girl whom I loved. I would have married her, but the world kept taking the girls I loved away from me.

I flew off to Omaha, Nebraska, to style hair for a fashion show. I had to teach a class of people who had 10 to 20 years more experience than I did. But I had a creative ability, and since I lived in LA, I was able to adapt and do things because I put myself in the position to do so. These people never left their homes, unlike me, so the opportunity wasn't there. When I read the feedback from the class, I was left heartbroken but learned a lesson about hair and youth.

October came, and I was styling hair again at LA Fashion Week. I really loved being part of the team, although I didn't get any of the spotlight they were filming, and I wanted to be in the spotlight. DNA salon was leading the show, and they were sponsored by Wella, which meant I was working for free again. Usually, I would gain something from doing hair for free, whether it was a new client or a new lead to work on a show or a shoot; something would come, so I kept doing this. I was still working for Planet Beauty, and they allowed me to have the freedom to go to special events. I was still booking some work through my regular modeling agency. I was booked to work the premiere of "Chasing Mavericks" at the Grove. It was nice to make 500$ for a night's work. But this is such a small amount of money. I always felt like, because I am not white, I would only book small jobs. I guess I should be grateful that I ever even booked any jobs, while there are people who never get to feel the way I do and did.

Halloween was coming around again, and I got booked to work for Zen Arts dancers, styling hair for them at this huge mansion of Mulholland in a gated community with houses over 10 million dollars. This was a kid's party, and it was the biggest party with so many dancers, games, and money spent. It was more than I made in like five years just for one night. It can really bring us down to earth when you realize that at 32, you are going to parties that kids in LA get to go to as guests at like 7 years old. Anyways, I dream of being able to do stuff like this for my kids, too. I want to make my future wife proud of me and have my little girl be able to have the best birthdays every year. I don't want to let my life fade away into nothingness. I have to continue to live and build my dreams. I cannot let drugs, sex, and drinking take away my hopes and dreams.

I stayed in LA for Thanksgiving and Christmas. I accepted an offer to fly to Dubai for a job working for a Posh Salon. The salon where I was working was located at the most amazing hotel in Dubai, the Burj Al Arab, and this was a dream come true for me. I have always wanted to leave the country for work, and this was a great way for me to experience the world. Doing hair has opened the doors to me for so many exciting jobs. I flew Emirates and stayed in my own room at the Address downtown.

I had the most amazing experience. The Burj Khalifa was right across the way from my hotel, and you can see it from the balcony. I went to a fashion show on the Palms for Germany's

Next Top Model. I was cast in a short film where they made a cast of my face for a zombie movie. I attended a white party hosted by the owner of Splash Clothing to celebrate the release of their 2013 Collection. Both the lady who flew me to Dubai and the owner of Splash had wanted to spend private time with me. Maybe I should have just been a slut till I found someone who could pay for my business dreams to come true. I was back home in time for New Year's celebration with my best friend, and we partied in Mount Olympus. I am writing this story because I will probably end up taking my life early. I deserve to be dead, as I am unlovable. I am a dark angel, and I want to kill myself. But I didn't kill myself. I just kept partying, hoping that one day, I would find love again and dream of having enough money to support the love of my life, and hope and pray that I don't make her want to leave me. It saddens me to think that even the best and most loving couples break up over time.

2013 in LA

The year ended with a bang, and now I had to sell my car for $500, which was all they would give me for it at CarMax. I bought a bike from Craigslist, and I was very humbled. My hair was getting longer, and I was still not in love with anyone. I know my drug and alcohol addictions come from the lack of love in my life. I seem to think the more I drink, the more likely I am to get laid. I don't know how to just make love. Every girl knows that we men want to have sex with them. I just don't get why they wait and hold out. I was in love with a girl named Tobi, who worked at a strip club on Sunset. However, she may not have known it. She was just a cocktail server. She was the perfect angel. When I found out she didn't want to be with me, I went to her club and bought a bunch of dances with the other girls. I was drunk, it wasn't a good idea, I'm sure she hated me for it, and it was a waste of money. All I really wanted in life was to find love again, just as I did with Amber. This red-headed model, named Faith, would have had my heart, too. I would fall in love with her and stay with her forever. I love redheads with blue or green eyes. I just want to eat the pussy all day long, and watch my BBD enter her pale ass. I love pale skin with freckles. This black girl, Monique, came to visit from NYC. She was a good girl, so we just smoked weed and chilled. She was really hot, though.

So, I was working at Planet Beauty on Fairfax, working a normal job making $13 an hour, and they had one chair in the back for me to color and cut hair for clients. I met this Russian girl who came in, and she had me do her hair. I could tell she liked me. I found out she was an escort. She was a real sweet-hearted girl. By nature, she was somewhat melancholic, and she yearned for a better life. I wanted to help her, so I offered to do a photo shoot with her and style her hair. Yes, we ended up having sex, and the pictures came out amazing. I started doing my community service for my DUI at Goodwill. Goodwill was smelly and hard to deal with. However, I had only 100 hours to do. My court case ended in October of 2012. I went to trial, and the Beverly Hills lady fucked me over in court. She made it so obvious that she was lying. This is why we are no longer friends. Although we became friends after that, we then lost touch again. See, what she did was say that she remembered me coming home that night, and every single detail about that night of the DUI. But then she forgot the day I moved into her house and forgot so many other details.

So, to make a long story short, I had to turn myself in to the Beverly Hills Courthouse in May and go to JAIL in DTLA at Twin Towers. My attorney got me a wireless breathalyzer instead of an ankle monitor like the one Lindsay Lohan had to wear. It was illegal for me to drink for one year. So, check this out: this wireless Breathalyzer was always with me, and I would receive a text message five times a day to breathe into the machine. It had an infrared light and a camera that would take a picture of me while I was breathing into the machine to make sure it was really me. I opted for this device instead of the anklet because I was filming movies, and I couldn't wear a device around my leg while I was shooting. I had to complete Mothers Against Drunk Driving in downtown LA. I had to enroll in an 18-month class in Hollywood and attend each Thursday at 6 pm. Wow, this was a tough class, but I made it over time, and I would ride my bike to class every time. I would ride my bike everywhere in LA because I hated waiting for the bus system. Plus, I figured it was a better workout. I attended a house party in the hills at the Pheed house, where I had the opportunity to meet Miley Cyrus, which was pretty cool. I just told her I loved her face. At the time, I didn't recognize her. I was still working with J-Beverly Hills, and we took a tour of the production facilities where they made all the shampoos and conditioners. It was amazing to learn that he married a woman who already owned all the production, and he was able to start making his own products. That was a smart way to build an empire. I was able to get booked on LA Talk LIVE, so I brought my best friends with me, and we had an hour on the radio show.

Valentine's Day was approaching quickly this year, so I had to go watch my girl, Nikki, perform in the valley with a company called Hells Bells. She was the lead girl. Then we went to the club after she changed in the car. She has the most perfect rack. She stayed the night at my house. I wanted so bad to keep her as my girlfriend. I was in love with so many girls, but Zoe Kush was particularly beautiful to me. She came to my house once, and it was great to meet her. Right around this time, I won my settlement with Zombie and Bitch. I received a large sum of cash, with which I was able to repurchase my computer which I am typing this book, as well as a professional camera, a 5D Mark II, to film and shoot for my website. I was shooting and I loved it. I shot Hannah and her best friend. These girls were like rock stars, both stunning with perfect bodies and flawless faces—one with red hair, the other with black. Finally, we went to the House of Blues on Sunset Boulevard to watch Steely Dan play. It was a good show. After that, my life got real fucking boring. I had a normal job, no car, and about $10,000 to my name. I was chasing white girls who did not love me, which is a waste of time. I seem to like bad girls. One of them was a blonde chick for the OC who was a porn girl. She was all about her money with long blonde hair and A cup tits. She would pay to have her hair done, which was cool.

I got a neck tattoo that says 'Dior' in Arabic. I was able to style hair for a concept movie at the studio that designed the moldings for the movies Predator, with Arnold Schwarzenegger, Aliens, and Mortal Kombat. Then my birthday was coming up, and I was really depressed. I made a list of girls' names that I was so willing to fall in love with, be loyal and have a relationship with. All these girls spent time with me, paid me to style their hair, or we would party and go to clubs together.

Here is the list of first names only: Nikki, Amber, Tobi, Cody, Chelsea, Kiesha, Carla, Kelly, Jess, Erica, Paloma, Eden, Anna, Brooke, Faith, Donna, Emily, Kim, Angel, Amanda, Nina, Nasia, Keeli, Sofia, Hayley, Kirra, Caitlyn, Mary, Britt, Melissa, Lizzy, Ally, Jennifer, Jen, and Katie. Somehow, I could not create a loving bond with these girls. What was I missing? How come love avoided my love? Is it because I lived in a studio apartment? Is it because I only had 10k to my name? Is it because I was insecure? Like, why do I have to have damaged girls that I repair, and those are the ones that love me? Is it because I did hair for a living, and I was not a stockbroker? The world was really bringing me down. All I want is true love. Right around my birthday, April 16th, I flew to Pennsylvania with my dad to visit his mother, who was about to pass away. The last time I was in Pennsylvania was when I was 2 years old.

I have no real relationship with any of my dad's relatives. We don't speak to each other, and we don't do anything, but this trip was very welcoming and loving. It was a pleasure to see my dad light up and be around his family. I got to see how small a town my dad is really from and how he is the only one who left and moved to California, sort of leaving the nest. I am first-generation in this country on my mom's side; my mom was born in Mexico City. I was flying back home on April 22nd, and my dad and I were able to stop in Philadelphia and have a cheese steak. I attended my first Lakers game on April 28th, which was pretty cool. I couldn't wait to sit on the court near the way of Kendall Jenner. So, in May, I'll come around and do a shoot with this Latin girl, who I think will be famous one day, whose name is Nat City. So here comes the time to pay the piper. I checked myself into the Beverly Hills courthouse on May 9th, 2013. Since I had long hair, I braided the sides into cornrows. Just in case I got in any fights, they couldn't pull my hair. As soon as I got to Beverly Hills, they called my name, and I went back into a small waiting cell as they handcuffed me and took my shoelaces. Then they transferred me downstairs to a larger holding cell, where I was in a room with all the other people being taken to the downtown Twin Towers, as they are called. One of the guys was a rapper with these dope shoes on, I forget the name, but they were dope. Another guy was busted for selling prescription drugs. He was a white guy from Beverly Hills, a cool guy. So, then they gave us peanut butter a honey sandwiches, so gross.

It was time to board the bus to the real jail after five hours of waiting. There were some nasty bums who were talking to themselves. Once we arrived at the Twin Towers, they put us in

146

a holding cell that kept getting more and more filled up with people. The temperature began to rise to a scorching and uncomfortable level. There were all these thugs in one room. Once they filled it with so many people, they finally let us out to be searched. They were very loud, strict, and mean. After being searched, we were all lined up and had to speak with someone to explain our job types and other details. I guess this is how they classify you and decide where to put you in jail, as if they put you with people of the same class type. After that long process, we 250 people were to shower and then change into the clothes they gave us.

I was the first one in the shower, but I was like, "Fuck that shit. I don't need a shower."

I was not getting naked around all these men. fuck that. We had to wait in that room for an hour; it was not the Four Seasons hotel in Maui. While I was in that first room, I felt like I was getting sick. We had to be processed more, so around 12 am, they asked if anyone was sick and wanted to see the doctor. So, I said, "Yes," which kept me from actually being put in the general population.

I got to stay in with the people who needed to see the doctor. It was so hard to fall asleep there. The bed was rough, an old man was snoring, and the clothes smelled and didn't fit. This was the third time I had been locked up for being drunk at one point. I needed to learn my lesson and never let this happen again. The next day, around 6 pm, I saw the doctor and asked him when my release date was. He told me it's in 10 days, which freaked me out. I think I went back to my room afterward and quietly shed a few tears under the blankets. I really felt like a loser. Why was it so hard to make money and have real love? I got the being healthy part down. I love to have fun and enjoy life. What was my problem? So, as the process continued, they asked me where I wanted to go. This meant they separated us by race. There are Blacks, Whites, and Mexicans divided into North and South, along with gays. I had to think about this. My name sounds white, and I don't speak Spanish. I thought that if I went to the Mexican side, they would force me into a gang for protection and ask me where I lived, and make me do favors for them when I got out of jail. So, I was like, "Fuck that, I don't want to be forced into a gang."

As for the white people, I figured they wouldn't really bother me because they didn't want me to be part of them anyway. So, I chose the white side.

They continued to move us from room to room to room all day long. I had to sleep another night in the Twin Towers. The next day, I was in the final waiting room before being transferred to the general population. I was in a small room that was filling up quickly with Arian looking skinhead white guys. I was starting to realize how not white my skin is. Even though I was born and raised in California, that doesn't mean shit; it's really just about the color of your skin. To my surprise, after waiting 8 hours in a room with 20 people, they called my name, and I was to be let go. This was on Mother's Day. So, it's another long process waiting to get out. Thank God for overpopulation. My crime was nonviolent, so I was the first to be released. I wore my Jordans to jail, which probably wasn't a good idea. This scary black guy threatened me that he wanted my shoes. He couldn't do anything while we were on the way out, but once we were outside, he could. It freaked me out, but nothing happened. On the way out, I ran into the white guy from Beverly Hills, and we shared a cab back to his place in Beverly Hills. He had this porn star girl, Angel Del Ray. I should have fucked her that day when I first got out of jail; she would love it. I just didn't know who she belonged to. I realized that girls who do porn are acting. They love sex when they are getting paid for it. It's the money that turns them on and the being naughty that they love. Most of them aren't down just for sex; they feel used when it's just sex. I mean, sure, there are some; it's both mutual sexual attraction, and that just takes more time to find. Sexual seduction is amazing, too.

So, I was out of jail and summer was coming up. I had purchased some Versace swimwear and left it in the bag on my bed, so when I arrived back home, I could have a present to open and feel wonderful about summer coming up in LA. So, Ash Hollywood's birthday was on May 25th, and she let me style her hair for her special day! We celebrated in Hollywood with a bunch of porn stars. It was pretty epic. You know, it's strange—porn girls are just normal people who enjoy acting on their sexual impulses. Coming from a Christian school gave me a lot of inhibitions, and to unlearn what I subconsciously think I should be doing for it to feel right, I either have to be drunk, high, or doing it as part of a job. I just want to be free and say and do as I please with no fear. That will all happen when I become an artist with financial means and create my dreams, like Andy Warhol. On June 25th, I cut my hair at Salon Heron in Hollywood. They shaved the sides all the way to the back for an edgy haircut. Planet Beauty probably didn't like my haircut. They seemed to hate that I was growing it out in the first place.

Around this time, I met a girl from San Francisco who knew some of my friends, and we hit it off because we were from the same town. She was a webcam girl and wasn't uncomfortable being naked for Playboy, so I offered to do a shoot at her house, and it turned out amazing. I loved it. We started dating and became very close; we spent a lot of time together, although we were both still single at the time. Around this time, I discovered a girl on Facebook whom I fell in love with. She was a girlfriend of one of my clients.

She had long, blonde, thick hair, a young, wild soul with creative energies, whom I would fall in love with in the future. Also, Christy Anderson lived around the corner from me, and I loved to hang out with her, even though she had many men paying for her. I was filming a documentary of girls and asking them questions about what it's like to live in LA. She was one of the girls I filmed, and she was candid about meeting men for dinner that they would pay her for dinner and sex. It seems that all the most attractive girls do this in LA. They don't have to work, and they earn more money in one day than most people do in a week of work. I hate this. It's not real. It's fucked up. Either legalize sex for money, or help girls get real jobs, or I don't know. It's just all the girls get jaded, and the men think they can just buy sex. It's like men don't need women for anything else besides sex in LA. My close friend, the one who introduced me to the lady in Beverly Hills, came to visit me in LA. She had lost a lot of weight and wanted to show off to me, but then say, "Oh, you can't have me now, I have a boyfriend."

I loved her, but I couldn't be in love with another stripper. I just can't deal with the late nights and the men who call during the day. It feels like they're all just acting and playing men for money. I took a trip to Las Vegas for the 4th of July, and that was a blast.

We stayed at my best friend's brother's house. We went to pool parties at night and pool parties at the Wynn, so many hot, sexy girls out in Vegas. I ran into Keeli, who used to live in SF. She was working at the Wynn as a bottle service hostess; they make a lot of money. Then we went to Haku San and got a table by the DJ booth. When we came back, I did this shoot out in the desert in July. The photographer didn't think this one through. It was 110 degrees or hotter, and we hiked a mile into the desert to shoot the scene. The photographer's girlfriend got a heat stroke, which was really rough. We got the shots, but it was a disaster getting home. I had brought an umbrella, and it kept me cool. I had to carry everything back to the car, and I saved my friend from passing out. We all drove back into town and needed to call an ambulance for one girl. When she got to town, she got naked in the store and poured water all over her body. She was losing her mind. The ambulance arrived, and they placed her inside. We were following them, and they pulled over. She went crazy in the ambulance, thinking they were abducting her. She broke free and started punching the staff, but her boyfriend managed to calm her down. It was quite a dramatic photoshoot. On July 19th, we took a trip down to San Diego for Comic-Con, which was an international event, so it was huge. It was like Halloween in San Diego. We went out at night to the nightclubs and had a really good time. I met a few new girlfriends who I still talk to today.

The night we came back to LA, we went to XIV, one of the craziest parties in all of LA, which was only open during the summertime. Coming back to LA and hanging out with my SF girl was pretty cool; she was the closest thing to a real relationship I've had in LA for a long time. I've dated girls for short periods of time, and this one seemed to last on and off throughout the entire summer. We both had jobs where we shared our sexual sides, so we fit well together, and she lived close to me. We even got lucky and ran into Rihanna at the hair shop on Wilshire together. I started working for this catering company, where I would bartend for extra money, making around $200 a day. This was amazing because it was extra cash, and I love bartending - meeting people and pouring strong drinks. We hosted one event up near Santa Barbara, located off Casitas Pass Road, and I felt really lucky to serve Heidi Montag and Spencer Pratt that day. I was still styling hair and had a shoot booked in downtown LA for a dress company through my friend Chels, who was my neighbor at the time. It was a good day; we had about five models that day, and it was for their website. I was working at the Bungalow Salon, now located on Beverly Blvd. I had new management at Planet Beauty, and my new boss hated me. She was like the mom on Bob's Burgers, and I told her that I didn't think she liked it. I was more of a stripper, model, porn star, actor, bad boy who liked to fuck in orgies and do cocaine all night and take shots of whiskey off girls' belly buttons. Who does hair for runway shows and young, pretty models?

Parents and kids should stay far away from me; we have nothing in common. As it was slow at the bungalow salon, I didn't have many of my own clients yet. So I went on Craigslist and found a casting for the show "Let's Make a Deal" with Wayne Brady. I got lucky; within an hour of sending the email, they wrote back to me and wanted me to come on the show. This just means I was a contestant; I still had to be chosen. On September 19th, I appeared on the show and was chosen at the very end to participate in the quick cash deal, which I unfortunately lost. So I came home that day with a broken heart lol. I begged the gods to show me a sign if you want me to be in LA. I was having a hard time accepting all the blockage and drama I was facing in life. So many loves yet no one loved me. I had to settle for less than what I wanted in all areas. Sure, shooting porn and having girls blow me and getting paid was great, but it was all so empty after it was over.

I pay $175 for a blood test and make $500 on the job. I get booked once a month. My big dick is just under 8 inches, and in order to make it in porn, you need money to blow. I was bigger than average and better looking than 9 out of 10 male porn stars. Most of the men are gross, and yes, it's the most racist business in the world. White people's porn is the most booked and watched; then you have black, and that's about it. Back then. A few Latin girls make it, and a few Asian girls, but very few Indian girls. I have seen them. Alina Li was one I got to work with. She was an amazing Chinese girl. You can check porn hub what is the most watched here in the USA. Anyway, my point is that even or especially in XXX, skin color matters; girls would get paid more to shoot with black websites because that was the lure, paid more. I was an extra on Star Trek, I shot a reality show for 24 hours on Playboy, and I was on Ellen for 1:30 seconds. I styled hair at the Playboy Mansion and modeled at the premiere of "Chasing Mavericks." It's all stuff I did, but I made less than $10,000 with all my work. God, please tell me I am better than this; tell me I will be chosen to be saved from a life of minimum wage slavery. The most money I ever made was winning a lawsuit. Secondly, I was given a few cars to drive, and I crashed all of them: two BMWs and one S500. I have 2 DUIs. All my girlfriends are strippers, models, porn stars, web cam girls - all bad girls. I have a star tattooed on my balls. Who am I? Please, LA, show me a sign that I should stay because I want to call it quits. The show called me back and asked, "Hey, would you like to be on? Let's make a deal again for our Valentine's Day show?"

I said, "Yes!"

Some time would pass, and my true love would return to my life on September 21st. She came. This is Amber. She wanted me to do her extensions, so I did them at my house. She had got more tattoos, and she wasn't the same girl I loved anymore. She lost a lot more of her innocence. Additionally, I was a small fish in a big pond in LA. It wasn't like San Francisco, where I knew all the people in the scene. She realized that all I am is a sweet-hearted guy who is off track and parties a lot, has no car, no real money for vacations, and I live in a studio apartment by myself. I wish we had made love that day. I wish she loved me. I didn't feel the magnetic attraction I used to feel. That same night, I went to play house where my friend Kiesha was working, and she and Amber looked so much alike. I was hoping I could have her love, and this would be it. My insecurity messed me up. I was 33 years old and I expected more of myself. I wanted a house with a business that earns me over $1,00,000 a year; that's what I need to feel like a man. All this shit has me feeling weak and spent. That's why sex and connection to a woman feel so important to me. I need connection, I need love; it heals my heart. It makes me feel loved, even though I haven't had the education I need to succeed in this world. I want to go to college, and I want my mom and dad to be there for me. I don't want to be a hair stylist; I want to be an actor or make television commercials. I thought I would become a famous porn star. That never happened. They don't care about a tattoo on my balls. It means nothing to anyone. None of my paintings will ever be worth money. Maybe when I am dead, they will be. I go back on the show and say, "Let's make a deal."

I have my 15 seconds of fame, winning $14,000 with a random contestant, and we split the money. This money will be my safety cushion. I have not had health insurance or dental for 7 years now.

All the money from the lawsuit was spent on rent, food, and some travel. I won't get the money till the show airs next year on Valentine's Day. The year is passing by so fast. One more trip to Vegas to film an independent film for $300. This job should pay $3,000 or $30,000, if this were a real movie. I'm getting fucked over. I have no real friends in the Hollywood acting game. While I was in Vegas, I stayed with my ex, Amber, and we got to go out like old times. She just didn't want to have sex with me. We slept in the same bed that night, and I wish she could love me again. I know if I were rich and successful, she would love to make love to me. Money is all that I need in this world, and the world doesn't want me to have it. Agents don't choose me; casting directors don't choose me. I get shit for pay as an actor, and it's because of racism in America. Racism was why I won that lawsuit for Zombie and bitch. It took four years to win, but they paid 20 million dollars across the board to all the people they were racist too. Amber ever told me that she couldn't marry me because if her/our baby, her child, weren't white, her family would disown her. That breaks my heart. So, it's November 20th, and I get to shoot with Alina Li, as I mentioned earlier. Her pussy was so tight that she made me cum too soon that day, so I had to wait like 20 minutes. I got to fuck her backstage to get hard again, and that sex was a golden memory. She danced for me solo, and I filmed it for myself. Little did I know that my high school buddy would see my shoot with Alina. He said I was the luckiest guy ever to be able to be with her. I felt happy that my regular male friends saw me as a STAR. I guess the experience is worth a lot, and I feel that.

Then Alina and I were back fucking on the movie, and I got to cum again for the cameras as she was blowing me. I love when girls eat my cum, it's so hot. Except cougars? No, I don't like that. On November 24th, I'm working with a German model, and we are going to shoot a commercial for Doritos chips because they hold a contest every year for a million dollars. If they choose your commercial to be aired during the Super Bowl, you win big time. This girl, Paisley, called me the same day, and she had impeccable timing. I should not have let her come that day, but because I was in love with her from the moment I met her, I couldn't say no to her. The German model Playmate Nasia and I had chemistry, and Paisley got in the middle and fucked it up. She was aggressive about what we were shooting, and she even took her little, amazing puppy with her, making the film about the dog rather than the girl, which everyone loves, especially the girl. I fucked up. I let this dumb bitch get in the way of my success. I let love fuck me over, and I don't fall in love. Amber was the last love I had. We filmed until sunset and came back to my house to edit.

We just missed the deadline for the submission to Doritos Super Bowl, because she was taking too long to edit. We ended up fighting about it. She knew a little more than me on Final Cut Pro, and I was just going to let her be and see what she was going to do. I gave her leeway. That was our first time spending time together. Paisley was my dream girl; I wanted to marry her. I love her hair, her eye color, she's not the pretty's girl in the world, she's not like Pamela Anderson, but I don't want a girl like that. I want an understated, down-to-earth love. I would fantasize about us starting our own production company and building a real future here in LA together. Deep breath, sigh. I drove up to the Bay Area for Thanksgiving this year. Sorry to say it, but I hated the Bay Area. I loved LA. It was so exciting. My family is great, and I do love them.

I just wish they had more drive to be creative and wealthy. By the time I came back, my edit of Nasia's bikini nun chucks had already hit 50k views. Not to mention, Paisley Dog Beau was not in the video. She really fucked it. I wasted an opportunity that I forgave her for. My good friend and client was how I met Paisley. She was the roommate, and it was Cody's birthday. I was invited. We celebrated in Hollywood, and Paisley was there again. We took pictures, and she was very kind and sweet to me. I was flirting heavy, and she was letting me be close to her. These are bad girls. They kiss, they drink, they shoot nude. They are my dirty angels. I don't feel guilty for fucking Alina Li's wet lips for the camera. We have an understanding. We all like to fucking party and get paid. December is already here now, and I get to meet one of the hottest girls one night out at the club. She was Latina and was wearing a red dress. I went to speak to her that night, and she said she couldn't leave the table she was at.

So, I was like, "Damn."

This club had dope fog machines, and when the music was pumping, they set it off. I got the urge to go steal the girl I picked up, and when the fog cleared, she was with me. I got her number, and we stayed in touch. Later, she would come over to my house, and she taught me how to smoke pot via dabbing. We had the best sex. It was so fucking good. I loved it. Around the 16th of December, I got a job working for the dry bar on 3rd Street. I had to have my friend come in for a blow dry, and I thought I fucked it all up, but they called me back and said, "When can you start the training?"

Woo-hoo. This was a new job, but it sucked. They had me work 40 hours a week, starting at 7 am, which meant waking up at 6 am and riding my bike to work. I do one last photo shoot this year in Beverly Hills, and then it's New Year's baby! We brought it in at the Park Plaza Hotel, and I met my New Year's date, Veronica. She looked exactly like a girl named Veronica from San Francisco, so I called her by that name, and she was like, "Yes?" Just happened to be her name, too. We stayed in touch, went out on a few dates, and it was pretty cool. My other fav girl was there, Christy Anderson, and she kissed me for New Year's!

2014

2014 was the year I realized that the world is rife with conspiracy theories. I realized that on the back of the dollar bill, the word Mason had a star-shaped pentagon in the circle over the pyramid of the all-seeing eye. I started to watch all sorts of documentaries about Freemasons and realized how far back this satanic ritual goes. People like George Washington were Freemasons. Almost every single American president is a Freemason. We are trapped in an un-American way of life.

***

I was asked to style hair for the Willian Morris Christmas party they hold in January. This was in San Diego, and it had a very cool circus theme. What a fantastic way to party, build a great company, and grow a brand. On January 9th, I was walking down Hollywood Blvd. when I noticed Jimmy Kimmel filming; they were asking people what their most interesting secret was. I offered my story for publicization, telling them that my first tattoo is a star on my balls/testicles.

They said that was interesting, but too much for TV. Anything else? Besides being a young porn star, I told them that I did over 50 bachelorette parties. They had to consult their producer, and later that night, I was featured in an interview on the Jimmy Kimmel show. I really feel like I have a similar story to Channing Tatum's. I am just not as lucky as he is to become an A-list celebrity yet, and I am not 100% white, which would help in Hollywood. I started training at the Drybar in Pasadena. I passed my training then I was off to Vegas. Vegas hosted the AVN Awards, and I was able to attend for free, receiving backstage passes. All my favorite porn stars were there, and I didn't have to pay to get in. I was really part of this industry. I was happy to see Riley Reid at the Evil Angel booth. When I walked up to see her, she remembered me, and she looked so sexy that day. What a lovely fantasy to be paid to have sex with her. Another gorgeous girl was Maddison Ivy. I had met her on set with Brazzers. I took pictures with Vanessa Veracruz; she liked me and would have loved to shoot with me, but we never got booked together. She did give me her cell number. My DVD poster was plastered high for everyone to see my work.

I got to reconnect with Trinity Saint Claire, whom I had met before she became famous, at a Halloween party in Hollywood, where she was best friends with Riley Reid. I got to meet Dillion Harper, whom I had a big crush on. Later in life, we got booked to shoot, and I was excited about that. My next girl, and she was one of my all-time favorites, was Veronica Rodriguez. I felt like we really needed to shoot together, and in a perfect world, we should have been set up. I had asked her if I could style her hair for the red carpet, and she said, "Yes," but in the end, her assistant never actually followed through. I'm sure it's because she had a boyfriend. She was growing really fast and doing very well. Dakota Skye was there, and we were really getting it on with flirting. She was then called back to her booth and yelled at the jelly producers; we needed to become friends that day, ugh. My close friend Riley Jensen was there at the white party! I also ran into Raven Bay, and all of us took pictures together. Raven Bay looked really hot. All this, and I would come back to my ex-girlfriend's house, Amber, in Vegas.

We went out the second night and ran into Aiden Ashley and Dave Nivaro. Of course, Amber knew Dave, and they went up to the hotel room to talk. She said they wanted to have a threesome, and God knows they probably did. I hate not being famous. I deserve the spotlight. I am a STAR. Let me shine, world. Give me the tools to spread my art and my heart. Riley Reid won awards that year and made my dreams come true because I got to have sex with her. I was flown to Vegas to shoot with her; it was a dream as far as sexual fantasy went. What do I have out of it? Just a DVD of me and her. She does give one of the best blow jobs I've ever had. I ran into Alina Li that weekend as well, and she was nice to me. She remembered me, too. She was with a group of amazing girls; all skinny and so fuckable. When I returned to LA, the next big event was the XBIZ Awards, and I was able to walk the long red carpet, which felt like I had truly arrived. I was able to see Veronica Rodriguez and take pics with her. She really liked me. I can't believe we never shot together.

My friend Amanda was my date that night; I couldn't have gone alone. Later, I ran into Raven Bay again. I still needed to shoot with her as well. That night Jenna Jamison was speaking on stage, and I just remember how trashed she was, and I never want to let myself go like that. Just because we have sex for fun doesn't mean we have to overdose on drugs and spend way too much. One day, I will be able to throw my EP production party after a worldwide search for the talent that will be showcased. I need funding, so I hope my book sells or I find an investor. I just need my own attorneys and licenses to build my dreams, which everyone will love and adore, Studio 54 Style. It will be a place of complete bliss and delight, and peace. All emotions will be precisely and clearly expressed and readily observable, leaving nothing to implication. I am a big fan of House of Cards, and I was lucky enough to go to the second season premiere at the director's guild on Sunset. I saw Kevin Spacey, one of my all-time favorite actors. This was on February 13th, 2014. The very next day, my episode would air, and I would have my biggest break in LA. I won $7,000, and I felt secure and safe. For the most part, I have money saved, and I'm not just living paycheck by paycheck. I'm not forced to be a stripper for anyone. I'm not forced to have sex for money with anyone. I can just live and work hard and safe.

I was talking to a new girl named Lauren Flare. She was shooting every day and was very busy, but her agent stole all her money, and she never came back. She deleted her contacts, and she was a rising star fast. She was an Aries just like me, but since that ended, I kept talking to this equally as trashy girl, Paisley. She was dating a meth using pimp, and he was damaging her beyond belief. I felt bad for her. I began studying the ancient Sumerians and realized that the Bible copied many of its original stories from this group of people. My religion faded away due to science. The fact that our Earth is one of billions of places that support life makes it obvious that we are not alone. March is already here, and I have been working at the dry bar blow-drying hair every day. I will never make a substantial amount of money styling hair for this company; I will just be making barely enough to stay afloat. I liked to go out on Saturday nights, and one Saturday night, I met soon-to-be playmate Miss September Stephanie Branton. I felt so lucky because she was incredibly beautiful, and she gave me her number, which is why I ended up living in LA. to make dreams like this my reality. She was from Canada and wanted to move her family out to LA. She would navigate the pool of rich men who would pay to make her dreams come true. Something I could not do, but she was still willing to be kind to me.

Can I just meet a beautiful girl a fall in love, please? As time went on, we simply became friends, and she became a playmate; we hardly spoke again. She took off, she grew wings, and flew out of my zone. This year flew by pretty quickly because all I was doing was working 9-5. This is when I started to get depressed. I didn't have a car, so I rode my bike to places. I had a little money, but nothing I felt safe spending it on. I paid for a photo shoot to get back into modeling and acting with Christian Rios, and my pictures didn't even make me happy; it didn't look like me. I wanted so much to have a normal life as an actor or model. I felt like I crossed the line, and now I was an anomaly in life. All I did then was work, and with my birthday coming up in April, my agent called to ask if I wanted to work with Adriana Chechik. That was one of the craziest shoots ever. I hardly ever speak about it. I've never seen a girl so beautiful and cock thirsty. It was amazing and weird at the same time. It is safe to say that Adriana took a load of cum in her back door. I was proud that I could do that with her, lol.

Later that night, my friends came to my favorite Mexican restaurant and we had dinner. I was really questioning my life, like, what has this come to? I made $300 today and exposed my innermost gift to the world, only to be unappreciated and unacknowledged. I was disappointed that I couldn't spend around $10,000 on my birthday and invite all my friends out to celebrate. I knew I wasn't the only one who wished to do something wonderful for his birthday, and being 34 at the time, I had expected more from myself.

June rolled around, and I got booked to shoot with Jezebel Vissor, which was such a fun shoot. All of this was porn star sex and nothing that was real love. I do remember sitting on Sunset Boulevard with a few tacos in hand, along with my two close friends, and we were eating dinner late at night. I see this girl walking down the street in a tight dress. She looked like a tall, skinny model, and she was walking along the street. I thought she was going to get in her car and leave. Turns out she was lost, and she came back up the street, and I had to go speak with her. She was an Australian girl on vacation. She seemed to like me and asked if we could go party and smoke pot.

I was like, "Sure." So, we went back to my house. I left my two friends at dinner and just hopped into a cab.

When we arrived at my place, she immediately took off all her clothes and started dancing to her favorite DJ, who was playing. My friend was staying with me, and I told him she came home with me. So, he came later; by then, we were already having sex. We had sex all over my house. She had a King Cobra tattoo on her back, which was large. She had no body fat and was the perfect dark-haired angel. She turned me on so much. We had sex nine times that night, all night. My friend decided to take his stuff and drive back to San Diego. We were having sex in the kitchen, and he was like, "You have fun. I've got to go." I could never make these fantasies come true if I had a girlfriend. I don't ever want to lie or cheat on any girl. All that hard work of waking up early and not going out, I guess, was rewarded with good sex on occasion. On July 3rd, my real dream girl came into my life, and we had sex for the very first time. We had a date at the grove, and we went wine tasting. Then we came home, and I licked her pussy for about 30 minutes. She had the best, cutest pussy I've ever seen.

I let her come on top of me. All 8 inches barely fit inside her, and she came immediately. All this water gushed out of her body. I didn't mind it at all. I was excited that it was my first time making a girl squirt. I had waited for this girl for so long, and if she came sooner, I would quit porn and just fall in love with her. When we were fucking, it felt so tight. It felt like I was trying to fit 8 inches into a 5-inch space. Yet, I had no idea how tangled the road we would take would become. Later that month, I was going to the doctor for a curable STD. She was a bad girl just like me, maybe even worse. She was deeper in bad drugs with bad people; like, how does she not know how to take care of herself? All the porn girls have to be blood tested before we can have safe sex. This was a tough situation to be in.

The 4th of July came, and we watched the fireworks in the valley after partying with friends. At work, I needed a hair model, and I had the beautiful Emily come into the Drybar. This girl will become famous one day. Needless to say, I was feeling empty. I had an incredible sex life, yet no love, and that's what I wanted more than anything, even more than money. Both money and love are tied together in LA. I gave my everything. I sold my soul for pleasure, and followed the dreams of my heart, and I was left feeling alone. I wanted to take a vacation to Ohio and meet a young girl who would be my girlfriend for 3-4 years, and she would probably leave me, as all young girls would. It's just what happens; people grow

165

apart. I wouldn't want that to happen, but I just had to prepare for the possibility that it might. So, as luck would have it, my other dream girl wasn't talking to me, and she told me later that she likes to fuck guys and then leave them. She didn't want to get attached. Now, it made room for a blonde girl from Ohio who was only 19.

She messaged me on Instagram and told me that she wanted to dye her hair. So, I met her at her place, and we started becoming friends by hanging out by the pool. We were talking about everything, and we seemed to fall for each other very quickly. Later that night, we were at my house, and I just started to play with her boobs, and she let me. We had sex twice that night, and I was a little alarmed that she seemed just to let me fuck her. She didn't have much emotion. We stayed friends and saw each other occasionally. On July 26th, I was booked to work Larry Flint's Hustler Mag's 40th anniversary party, where we were joined by models, and my ex-girlfriend was also in attendance, working. We had broken up, but we were still nice to each other. I met the beautiful Stacy Carr that night. Scarlet Red was the cover girl. Leia Cinn and I danced the night away. All the girls were naked and body painted, and they set me up with 10 different naked girls all night, rotating them in and out of bed with me. We could do anything besides have sex. At the end of the night, we were all playing on one bed. There were twenty girls and two guys were licking pussy and eating asshole.

I remember sharing this girl with Stacy Carr. I loved how she looked when licking pussy, She loved girls so much, and she was such a sexual beautiful girl. Time was flying by, and when I looked up, there were about 200 people. All of them were watching us and taking pictures, as if it were a huge orgy. It was amazing, but it sort of freaked me out, and I left before I was the last one on the bed. This would be one way to forget about the girl I loved, and who knows what she was doing; she was doing just as Naughty things as I was.

I took an internship working for this acting agency every Tuesday. I would come in for a couple of hours and see how a real acting agency worked. I could see the jobs that would come in for casting. It seemed like 20-30 jobs were being shot every day in LA. The money was incredible, $10,000 for a day's work—just reading a few lines for major corporations. I felt like shit; I'm licking pussy for fun, and the money barely does anything for me. It's pennies, it's nothing like the big-time jobs. I fucked up. And this is why I want you never to give up. I gave up once. I experienced racism, and I never thought I would get a fair shot at the good life—good work, good acting gigs, good movies, and good TV shows. Even working for a major agent, they did not represent me, and I was working for free. On August 8th, I went to see the Monster Tour with Slim Shady and Rhinna. It was all the way in Pasadena at the Rose Bowl. I was shocked to see all the fans. They all had a similar style, very ratchet.

I'm sure that the people who will read my story will be a diverse group. I hope that the men who read this will realize that working hard and earning money is crucial; without money, nothing else falls into place for long. Women are the only ones who really make any money in the sex business. Having a sugar momma was not the business; she was a nightmare. How was I going to win the heart of the love of my life and have her accept me? September comes, and my friend Stephanie now has worldwide recognition; that's all I ever wanted. I want to explain my story because one day I will be dead. I don't know how long I can last in this loser lifestyle with no true love. I received my check from Hustler for $300, and I remember that it meant nothing. All I was doing for the next couple of months was working at the Drybar. One of my managers asked me if I was gay or straight, and I told him, "If you can't figure it out, then I've done my job."

I hate that question, and it's none of their business. As a hairdresser in LA, women can be bitchy; they seem to dislike straight men, our feelings, and our opinions.

While at the Drybar, I'd meet new girls every day, and I wish I could just talk candidly with all of them. The problem was that other people were listening right next to me. As a straight man, women will have their guard up. However, with a slight change in tone of voice, they will assume I am gay, not knowing that I am a bachelorette party dancer, model, and pornstar who loves sloppy blowjobs and anal sex from girls like Alina li and Riley Reid. They didn't seem to mind if they thought I was gay, and all the craziness that happened in that world. They seemed to welcome gay men and hate straight men; the only ones they could tolerate were their husbands, and barely at that. So, I didn't need my boss asking me questions. I could act however I chose, and all of LA was a stage. I did my time in SF, and I was out of that world.

No one could judge me. I loved myself, and I worked hard to live and thrive as a survivor in that city. So, I finally got my wish, and my Ohio girl moved in with me. She was an angel for a month, and Halloween was coming up. We went to different parties that day. She had her own agenda; she just needed a place to live. She didn't want to date me.

That night, I went to 1 Oak and stayed out all night, missing work at the Drybar. I was starting to hate working there; my body was hurting, and I wasn't cut out to just blow-dry hair for a living. I got my agent back, Bud Lee. I was in great shape, with a really good body: a super six-pack. It was funny how LA worked. I was out at the clubs, talking with girls at HYDE. What happened was I would see a pretty girl come up, start talking, say, "Hi, my name is Jason."

They looked at me like, "So what?" They were thinking, "Who the fuck is this guy?"

She would say, "Where are you from? What do you do?"

I'd say, "I'm a hairstylist," and then she would look the other way, as if I were bothering them, and they would tell me to go away. I would then say, "Are you an actress? Do you have an agent?"

They'd say, "Yes," but they usually wouldn't have an agent!

I would say, "I'm a talent scout," and then their whole demeanor would change. Their eyes would open up, their body language would turn towards me, and they'd become super excited. It was messed up, but I would get paid if they could actually pass the audition process. I knew none of those girls would really be my friends; they would just take what they could and move on, like vampires.

Living with this girl from Ohio was kind of nice, and we hooked up occasionally, but she was a wild girl, and I liked that for the most part. So, I started looking for a new job, and I came across Sally Hershberger salons. I dropped off a resume, and the next day they had me come in for an interview. I asked my girl to fuck, so when I went into the job interview, I would be glowing, and she let me in. I hardly ever came inside, girls, but that day I did, and it felt so good. Of course, I got the job, and I was to start working with them as soon as possible. I was working with Mathew, and he was a gay man who seemed to think I was attractive. What I learned in SF, I had to take with me to LA. I wish I was working with a girl named Bianca. I wanted to be part of the young crowd, and I was so nervous. It reminded me of working for Di Pietro Todd in San Francisco. After I got the job, I had to live alone again. I couldn't be worried about what was happening at my house while I was at work, so I had Sav move out. I was sort of in love with this girl, but she was wild being an escort, and that was okay. I just couldn't handle it and work for this A-list Salon.

I had a lot to juggle. I was riding my bike to the gym as fast as I could one day to meet her and bring her a mixed CD. I ran through a red light, and I got pulled over in Beverly Hills; the cop wrote me a ticket on my bike. I could not believe it. People from my new salon drove by and saw me getting a ticket. On Tuesdays, I was still at the talent agency, scouting people as I could and learning how the real industry worked. I was still shooting XXX videos once in a while. I figured that because I was working in a predominately gay industry, I didn't make enough money to have the girl I wanted to be with be with me. I might as well allow myself to have some fun and live my childhood dreams. I felt like a badass. On Nov 18th, we celebrated a birthday for a girl I was so in love with, and I fucked it all up by getting drunk. I may have shown everyone the star tattoo on my balls. I woke up feeling incredibly hungover, but I still managed to make it to work. I started panicking, and I created an alter ego to fit in because I knew the men would accept me there.

I just fucked up my whole chance of being respected. This was two weeks in. I am a star, and I have talent, and I will succeed. I just need to be heard and loved. Please, world, love me.

My mom came to LA to visit before we flew to Mexico to celebrate my grandpa's 80th birthday. We stayed for 11 days and had the time of our lives. I did get sick the last day, and I did go to the strip clubs and spend money. Those girls were so hot. We watched the sun set and the fireworks, and I filmed the whole experience. Christmas came, and New Year's, and all I was doing was working and being good. I attended my boss's Christmas party at his house. My favorite friend and client came with me. She was truly beautiful. For Christmas, I received a Versace belt and glasses to complement my work style. We spent the New Year at Warwick, and I saw another love of my life on the way in. It was her birthday that day. That night passed quickly and uneventfully, which I was okay with because I couldn't handle any more bad luck from having fun.

2015 LA

Here's my 2015 story, though it's a bit heartbreaking. Robin Bunny flew in from Ohio, and her boyfriend was acting like a jerk, so she left him and stayed with me for a while before her flight back to Ohio. I sort of saved her from a bad situation. On January 22nd, I got to hang with the girl I let myself fall in love with foolishly, Paisley. We had a good time at Davey Wayne's Hollywood. It was so good to see her. She was a wild soul like me, afraid to love. That next weekend, I was out at The Nice Guy and met three amazing girls who came with me to 1 Oak. Later, I met another group of gorgeous girls, one of whom had a nickname, 'Pizza.' She was such a gorgeous girl. She was bound to become famous. I was able to get one of my amazing girlfriends signed to my talent agency in January, so in return, she booked me as a hair stylist for this photo shoot. I was able to work with an amazing makeup artist, Patrick Ta, and playmate of the year, Dani Mathers, along with Chelsea P. and other very beautiful models.

A couple of days later, I was at The Nice Guy again, and Drake was there. We stayed late that night. He had a private party, and I was late to work at Sally Hershberger the next day. But come on, they should have been proud of me; meeting Drake and getting to shake his hand added value to me as a hairstylist. Super Bowl came around, and the girl I love was being a weirdo and all caught up in her drama. I found a replacement girl, and she was not capable of really getting my love. She was a little bit younger, which didn't matter. It's just that she was willing to be with me anytime, anywhere, doing anything. Valentine's Day came up, and I spent it with her, even though that's not where my heart was. I got a blood test, and I was scheduled to shoot with Hope Harper, a cute little spinner girl from Florida. She wasn't supposed to let me, but she let me do this fun activity. We had a great shoot, and later that week, I got to shoot with Ash Hollywood. I had a variety of girls in and out of my life, and now that I'm almost 35, I just want to be in love. Yes, I want sex and good sex, but I want personality and I want a career. That's why I am working like a slave at Sally Hershberger salon. Along comes March, and my baby love and I are finally spending more time with each other, Paisley.

I want to let my heart fall in love. I want to be a good man. I want to be a boyfriend who is loyal, and I've already done all my wild shit. I just want to make one girl happy. Little did I know she wanted many men, and she just wanted to have sex. She should have just fucked me more often then. She was the reason I'm taking the time to understand myself and open up more to the world. I've exhausted all my other ideas in life. I don't have the money to go to school/college. I can't bear to be someone's sugar baby and have them pay for college. I don't have my family that can support me, and if this story saves anyone's life from making the same mistakes I have, then I will be pleased.

At the hair salon, I was shampooing Lisa Rinna and Jane Fonda. I once saw Martha Stewart arrive, along with the legendary singer John Mayer. This was where I thought I would stay working for the next 5-10 years. I was able to have my celebrity clients come in. I styled their hair, and people like Lexi Ainsworth for her movie premiere, "A Girl Like Her." I quietly slaved away for as long as possible, staying as nice as I could, gradually revealing my personality. All I ever wanted was to be creative and special and travel the world working for a great business. My birthday was coming up, and I wanted to go to Coachella for the first time ever. So, we left last minute and drove up there with no tickets and just talked our way into everywhere. The neon party was the best part of it all. I was able to meet Chris Brown, and he took a selfie with me. This was on April 12th, and on April 13th, I was strolling through Beverly Hills and the lady with whom I used to live had to sell her house, and she moved to Burton Way. I called her to stop in and reminisce about old times, and we had champagne and talked. It was pretty nice. She then called and yelled at me for not inviting her out to my birthday dinner. I finally told her exactly how I felt, and she was so hurt that we never spoke again. She was always holding her power over me, and I had already gone to jail and was fired by one of my bosses at Sally's that day. I had no patience to deal with her expectations. Back then, the Game was still developing. This was before OnlyFans and the whole world turning into "Entertainment only."

I was working with a Latin guy who was exactly the opposite of everything I was. He was so square and quiet; I was a firecracker who was wild, crazy, and independent. I had dinner at The Nice Guy's with my boys, and every year my birthday got smaller and smaller. I wanted success, and then I would have a reason to be happy. April 26th arrived, and I was scheduled to shoot with a company I had always wanted to work with. This was the craziest xxx shoot.

They call and say, "Can you work this day?"

"Yes, but who am I working with?"

This girl was married, which is a huge turn-off to me, and she was on her period, not to mention being sick. We were to shoot on a moving bus with Craigslist's $50-a-day extras; it was crazy. I normally don't take dick pills, but that day I should have. I called my agent and was like I can't do this shoot. It was too crazy. So, they switched me to another girl, and I was already traumatized and could not get hard to save my life, even though the girl was pretty hot. If I could choose the girls I work with, I would always have a great scene. They don't give us any choice; it's so weird. I did meet Karmen Bella, the prettiest Indian girl I've ever met in porn. We went out to see the movie "Entourage" together, and I took a picture and posted it on IG. One of her friends called her and was hating on me.

She stopped returning my calls, and I finally saw her at a party one day and was like, "What happened?"

She told me this guy that she met on a porn set said I was a horrible person. I've always been nice to everyone and lived an adventurous life. I could not believe he had ruined my friendship. She was a freak, and he lost the love of his life, and will never recover from it. At the end of that month, I went up on stage for the first time to try standup comedy. I love stand-up comedy and plan to have my own 1-hour special soon. It may come true, and my dream girl will be in my life. She knows my story about my sexual adventures, and we both have overlooked each other's downfalls. She gets paid to escort her time in K-town for the karaoke bars, and she has an older man who acts as her sugar daddy, paying for her dinners and trips to Vegas. I thought she would fall into place like Amber did when we both had similar lives. I started to shoot for a website and make money on the side, meeting girls who didn't mind posing nude or seminude.

I must say, it's a lot of fun watching girls take their clothes off. I love women so much. My love leaves for Europe with her Sugar Daddy, and my heart breaks, but I'm happy for her that she gets to see the world because I would have paid for it if I could; I just can't yet. While she's gone, I had one wild ride. I was driving from Santa Monica back to my place and was going so fast, it was like GTA or something. This ex-girlfriend came back into my life, and we ended up having sex in the Ralphs bathroom after speeding on the freeway and side streets. We were so drunk, and maybe it's because I was emotionally unavailable that all these girls were into me. But all I wanted was the one girl my heart opened up to, Paisley.

I flew back home to San Francisco and got to see Sara James, who was now going to UC Berkley and had moved on to a better life. I was still making minimum wage, partying like a rock star, hoping and praying for love. When I came home, I met Isabelle, a cute little blonde girl whose sex felt like heaven. She was such a good little girl; she needed head shots, and we shot her. I had to have sex with her. She was such a little flirt and was twerking in my bedroom. Her pussy got so wet. She was also an escort. She was a wild child. She had no rules, and I knew that I could not build a real relationship with her. She was too young in spirit.

EDC Vegas came around, and my true love and I went to Vegas. We filmed it all; that was our plan. She threw me some curveballs. She had met a guy and was talking to him as if she wanted to hook up with him. I had talked to no girls that way

176

when I was with her; it was just us. I should have been a dick and talked to as many girls as possible in front of her to make her jealous. That's the kind of girl she was. Although we came home together, and when we fell asleep and were cuddling, I felt so high off of her, and I told myself she was the one girl I wanted to marry. It only got worse from here. The more I loved her, the further she would run away. I was having sex with everyone but her; she was the only one I wanted. What kind of twisted hell did I enter? She didn't communicate like a normal human being. We kiss, we sleep together, but she didn't want to fuck. She was killing me.

I shot another girl for the website, and she was this amazing Asian girl who was also a stripper. She was so nervous, and she was begging me to have sex with her. It was so good. I loved the pictures, and she told me she could no longer see me. She said that she would fall in love with me if she did. I guess that's a thing girls don't want to fall in love. Suppose they sell their bodies in any way. I was able to fly to the Catalina Islands with Paisley's SD I took two girls with me, which was fun. He was trying to marry a lady and start a family. He just wasn't good-looking. He liked white women, and they made it extra hard for him, even though he was rich, smart, etc. I was an extra on a porn set, and one of the other girl extras gave me a ride home. We smoked weed. Then she gave me the best sloppy blow job ever, and I fucked her. She was like 19, Kasey Warner. I have pictures of her at my house. She had a nice hairy bush, too. August first was my next shoot, and this was when I got to fuck Dillion Harper. This was a long time coming. I really always liked her; she had the best tits. She doesn't do anal, but my cock slipped into her booty. It was a surprise she let me do it.

We shot this in a huge mansion, and it was in virtual reality. That was my last shoot since then. Because I wanted to be in this relationship, I realized it wasn't happening because I was living like a playboy. So, I told my agents to remove me from the booking list, and I was no longer getting booked. I realized this was not going as planned with me and my love, so I tried to break it off. I tried so many times just to end it. I colored my hair purple to fix it. It didn't work. I was in love with a girl who was like a best friend to me. I wanted to talk with her every day. I wanted to be there for her in every way. I was ready to give up all my ways and dedicate my time to her only. Halloween came around, and we had a bad Halloween. Christmas came, and she was out of town. I stayed in LA. We spent New Year's together, and it was just as bad. My whole world revolved around her. We kept spending time, and she never gave me the love I wanted; it shattered me. The one day we did hook up, she squirted, and thank god I have this memory. It was a piece of heaven to me.

Our Valentine's Day was so bad. She didn't know how much she hurt me. I got fired from Sally because they said I had an issue. Sally Hershberger, herself, needed a new assistant, and I offered to be it; she accepted the offer. However, her number two in charge told her I could not be it. They had filmed the Beverly Hills housewives at the salon, and I should have been there that day, but I was let go a week later. They never told me why. It was because they didn't like straight male porn actors. I found a new job quickly and was working in

Beverly Hills. I had a bruised ego, yet I was still working. I professed my love to her, and she wasn't willing to let me into her heart. She needed to be single to get rich or get jobs and not hurt anyone's feelings. Looks like she will be single forever.

She said, "I would have sex with you more often if you didn't say you love me, Jason."

At the moment, we are not on speaking terms, and I do not have a girlfriend. I am writing this book, and I've caught you up on my story. I pray that I have good news to share one day. I booked a flight to London and bought a car, and am back on track to living my dreams with or without her. I am working out and am stronger than ever before. I wanted to write this book and have it turned into a movie, so now I am on a mission to rebuild my life and have a normal, wild life, leaving my old ways for my future life. I want to stay sober and tell my story to help others live a good life. Feel free to request the next chapter of my life. I started writing the second book already.

Conclusion

Wow, what a life. I miss it. I've always wanted to die young. I want to be an artist and express myself. I need this book to sell. I need this book to turn into a movie. I want to explain the details on TV and all over the world. We have mixed feelings about it all. I know so few people who have done what I have done. It's not new; it's actually something you need to experience to know that sitting home alone can be a good place to be, not in jail, where one of my friends is now. I would rather be home alone in LA than in jail. I'm working 6 days a week for a clean energy company right now. I don't have a girlfriend, and I'm in a slump. No girl I love loves me back. The bad ones need money, and the good ones are afraid of me. My past shines through in my soul of trust. I love open sex, and I love relationships filled with love. I want both. My best friend is now a reborn Christian, which I was when I was a kid.

I need to buy a house, I need one girl to love me, and I need a cat and a dog and solar panels and an electric car. I need to write the next 10 years of my life to share my experiences. Do I settle down? Do I die young? I work six days a week, and I miss more than anything the love of someone I care about. My ex is about to have a baby. All my dreams fail if this book fails. I want to liberate so many young people. I want to liberate all the old people. I would live my life exactly the way it is; I would not go back and change it. I just need to make sure the future comes to me the way I need it to be. I love my new job and I am doing really well at it. I have everyone laughing and saving money. I love talking with people. I am here to help in anyway I can.

Thank you all for reading. Goodbye. Did I ever tell you about that week where Sav moved back in and we raged for 7 days straight lol? To be continued and questions answered only on IG or TV SHOW!! Jason Cool.

www.ingramcontent.com/pod-product-compliance
Lightning Source LLC
Chambersburg PA
CBHW051153120626
46547CB00012B/1062